HE'S *Almost* A
TEENAGER

Books by Peter & Heather Larson and David & Claudia Arp

$10 Great Dates: Connecting Love, Marriage, and Fun on a Budget

10 Great Dates: Connecting Faith, Love & Marriage

He's Almost a Teenager

She's Almost a Teenager

Other Resources From David & Claudia Arp

10 Great Dates to Energize Your Marriage (book/DVD curriculum)

10 Great Dates Before You Say "I Do" (book/DVD curriculum)

10 Great Dates for Empty Nesters

52 Fantastic Dates for You and Your Mate

The Second Half of Marriage (book/DVD curriculum)

Answering the 8 Cries of the Spirited Child

Fighting for Your Empty Nest Marriage (with Scott Stanley, Howard Markman, and Susan Blumberg)

The Connected Family

No Time for Sex

Suddenly They're 13—Or the Art of Hugging a Cactus

Other Resources From Peter & Heather Larson

The Couple Checkup (with David H. Olson and Amy Olson-Sigg)

10 Great Dates Before You Say "I Do" (DVD curriculum)

Great Dates Connect (DVD curriculum)

PREPARE to Last (DVD curriculum with David H. Olson and Jeff & Debbie McElroy)

PREPARE/ENRICH: Customized Version (inventory/assessment with David H. Olson)

Couple Checkup (inventory/assessment with David H. Olson)

HE'S *Almost* A
TEENAGER

ESSENTIAL CONVERSATIONS
TO HAVE NOW

Peter & Heather LARSON

David & Claudia ARP

BETHANY HOUSE PUBLISHERS

a division of Baker Publishing Group
Minneapolis, Minnesota

© 2017 by Peter Larson, Heather Larson, David Arp, and Claudia Arp

Published by Bethany House Publishers
11400 Hampshire Avenue South
Bloomington, Minnesota 55438
www.bethanyhouse.com

Bethany House Publishers is a division of
Baker Publishing Group, Grand Rapids, Michigan

Printed in the United States of America

Library of Congress Cataloging-in-Publication Data is on file at the Library of Congress, Washington, DC.

ISBN 978-0-7642-1137-9

Some names and identifying details have been changed to protect the privacy of those involved.

Contains material adapted from *She's Almost a Teenager* by Peter and Heather Larson and David and Claudia Arp (Minneapolis, MN: Bethany House Publishers, 2015).

Cover design by Faceout Studio

Authors represented by and this book is published in association with the literary agency of WordServe Literary Group, Ltd., www.wordserveliterary.com.

17 18 19 20 21 22 23   7 6 5 4 3 2 1

This book is dedicated to our sons. Thanks for being such great sports and giving us so many stories to share with others. You are a gift from God and we treasure who you are and who you've become.

Thanks to all the parents and grandparents who have gone before us. You give us hope, encouragement, and direction.

CONTENTS

INTRODUCTION

Welcome to the Tween Years: Let the Conversations Begin!

One mom overheard her eleven-year-old son, Sam, proclaim to his friend, "She's so hot!" as they discussed the popular girl from their sixth-grade class. Had puberty just begun? Was it okay that he had started to notice girls? Was it okay for him to talk about girls this way? Was it time to batten down the hatches?

Too often our sons' tween years are like a journey through a huge dark forest in which it is easy to get turned around, misdirected, and lost. But don't panic. Help is here, both for Sam's parents and for you. In the following pages we will help you prepare for and launch your son into adolescence. As you probably remember from your own tween and teen years, this can be quite a ride. It won't be perfect or smooth every day, but we hope to arm you with some helpful thoughts and direction for the journey ahead. First, let us introduce the team who will be your coaches on this trip into the world of adolescence.

Meet Heather and Peter Larson

We are right here with you on this journey with tweens and teens in our home. As parents of two daughters (Anna, age twelve, and Kate, age fourteen) and a son (AJ, age fifteen), we have treasured taking the time to write and talk through these essential conversations in our own family. Peter is a clinical psychologist and Heather is a life coach. Once upon a time, Peter was a youth worker and Heather taught fifth grade. We've had a lot of experience with children and have combined our professional and personal experiences to offer guidance and insight throughout this book. Gathering input from other families and working with Claudia and David Arp has been a blessing to us and will be an encouragement to you as well.

Meet Claudia and David Arp

We have three adult sons! For many years we have helped parents launch their sons and daughters into adolescence and navigate the sometimes turbulent teenage years. We founded PEP (Parent Encouragement Program) Groups for Parents of Teens and wrote the book *Suddenly They're 13—Or the Art of Hugging a Cactus.* We look forward to sharing our own experiences of parenting three sons and enjoying our five adolescent grandsons.

For this journey, Peter and Heather will be leading the way, as they are in the middle of the adolescent years. You can be assured that they understand where you are and you'll easily relate to them. Peter's training as a psychologist and Heather's as a former teacher and current life coach are invaluable in giving helpful advice and support.

We will be the behind-the-scene supporters and from time to time will share some "Arp Adages"—tried and true principles—as well as practical tips from other parents who have successfully navigated this passage. Years ago Dr. James Dobson helped us prepare for this stage of life in his classic book *Preparing for Adolescence.*

The four of us are standing on the shoulders of those who have gone before us. The Arps especially appreciate the wise counsel and advice from educators Bill and Kathy Clarke, who encouraged us to keep the lines of communication open and build the relationship with each child, and from Phyllis Stanley, who first shared the concept of preparing for the teen years through the vehicle of the Teenage Challenge (our Project Thirteen).

Our team would not be complete without you! You'll be amazed how much wisdom and insight you already possess. You may be part of a couple, a single mom or dad, or a grandparent who is parenting your grandson. Whatever your situation, you might want to pull others into your support circle. You can use this book in a small group with friends who also have tween sons and challenge them to experience these important conversations with their boys as well. As parents, you can share your successes (and redos when things don't go as planned) with each other.

You will discover that you are not alone in this process. You will also learn that each stage your son will go through is temporary and that each stage is leading to maturity! Thank goodness there is light at the end of the adolescent tunnel.

Why Conversations?

One truth that continues to rise to the top is the importance of the relationship you have with your son today. Although this book is for you as the parent to read, our hope is you will have new questions to start a dialogue with your son about the upcoming teen years. A conversation is an opportunity for you to be curious and really learn more about who your son is and who he is becoming. This isn't a typical parenting book with a "do this and expect this" kind of formula.

Instead, the following chapters include eight meaningful conversations or activities, each crafted around a topic of interest to discuss with your son. These conversations are designed to help you both get ready for the years ahead. Reading the chapter will help you, the parent, prepare for an activity or conversation to have with your son. We will look at the developmental process, biblical guidance, and plans for shifting more responsibility to your son as he matures. And for each conversation we will provide questions and talking points for meaningful discussions together.

Conversation 1: The Big-Picture Talk

You'll talk about the shift that will be taking place and how over the next few years your son will go from childhood to being a teenager, and finally to adulthood. Together you'll talk through goals and the changing roles each of you will experience in the upcoming years.

Conversation 2: The Friends Talk

This conversation will focus on your tween's natural shift in priority from family to friends. You'll have an opportunity to define together who he is becoming and talk about the importance of good friends.

Project Thirteen

Project Thirteen celebrates the arrival of the teen years with a creative opportunity for your teen to accomplish meaningful growth. Together, you'll craft a project designed to challenge your son to stretch himself as he meets specific goals.

Conversation 3: The Body Talk

This conversation will help you navigate the upcoming wave of hormones sure to hit your home. You'll talk about body changes, brain development, emotions, attractions, and how boys hit their growth spurts at different times.

Conversation 4: The Technology Talk

In our culture, many parents are confused about the differences between rights and privileges. This chapter gives you a formula for how to handle technology (or any other privilege) using a series of questions to help you clarify the responsibilities and expectations associated with these privileges.

Conversation 5: The Faith Talk

Faith is the most important piece of who we are and informs so many of our decisions. Your son will soon own his personal faith journey. Together you'll explore his plan for continuing to grow in his faith.

Conversation 6: The Academics Talk

Together identify academic goals for your son during the teen years. Discover his strengths and challenges, and plan together how to help him grow and reach his goals in school.

Conversation 7: The Girls Talk

Even though girls may not be a big topic yet, they soon will be! This conversation gives you both an opportunity to talk about the purpose of dating and describe the "dream girl." There are several thoughts to help your son stay pure in an over-sexualized culture.

Conversation 8: The Money Talk

One piece of independence is finances. This chapter will give you questions to help you discern your son's awareness of money and handling finances. You'll discuss expectations for future financial responsibilities and begin discovering your son's financial personality.

The Birthday Box Project

This final chapter pulls it all together with a great way to map the transition from tween to teen to adulthood. The Birthday Box provides a clear road map for progressively releasing more freedom and responsibility to your son each year in several significant areas.

What's the Best Format? Weekly? A Weekend Away?

What's the best approach for you to initiate these conversations with your son? This depends on you and your son's style and personality. Some of you may find that a structured weekly activity works well. For others, a weekend away together is a great time to discuss the conversations introduced in the book. Perhaps you prefer a more casual dinner conversation time by picking a question each week to introduce to the entire family with more personal conversations to follow.

What if your son is not cooperative? You're thinking, *He'll roll his eyes if I even suggest a meaningful conversation.*

Know your son. Some children like the formality of a special date. Others think it's corny or may feel like a "big talk is coming." Some parents will choose to read the book and be ready to

ARP *Adage*

Times with your tween son can be bonding times that help you focus on your relationship and convey the message that you are excited your son is growing up.

discuss the topics as they naturally surface in daily living. The topics are core to most tweens' experience, so you won't have to wait long before they begin coming up. In fact, portions of this book mirror what we cover in our book for parents of girls, *She's Almost a Teenager*. One parent said, "I knew if I wanted my son to cooperate, I'd have to make it really low-key. With him, I never used the term 'special date' or labeled the time as a tween conversation. Instead I would use opportunities to ask questions when we were alone in the car or doing an activity together."

Get Started!

Your tween is quickly becoming a teenager. Fear not, help is here. Unlike other parenting books, there will not be a one-size-fits-all approach. Instead, you'll be challenged to think through questions and see how your answers fit you, your family, and your unique and wonderful son. Make it work for your family. If you feel the need to rephrase the questions so they fit your situation better, go for it. Write down your own thoughts and notes in the margins as you read through each chapter. Decide what topics, questions, and conversations you want to use. If something in this book doesn't fit your circumstances, feel free to skip over it. We want this to be helpful to you and your son and not feel like a forced or contrived experience. Our prayer is that these essential conversations will set you and your family up for success and joy during the teen years and beyond.

Conversation 1

• • •

THE BIG-PICTURE TALK

Begin With the End in Mind

"Where is my sweet little guy? Who has taken up residency in his body? I don't recognize this new attitude! He doesn't listen and seems to question everything we ask him to do. It's a full two years until he is a certified teenager, but all I get is a grunt when I ask him about his day. What will the teen years be like? Any help out there?"

Nervous parents are realizing the "golden years of childhood" are ending earlier and earlier. Their precious eleven-year-old is beginning to show symptoms of adolescence. They're scared. They feel unprepared. They're panicked and don't know how to prepare for the coming storm.

One parent we spoke with gave an excellent challenge: "If you feel uncomfortable, embrace it!" In the following pages, we want to help you embrace the coming years and develop your own balanced approach to guiding your son safely into and through the teenage years and into adulthood. In each chapter we will frame questions to help you evaluate where you are in your relationship with your tween son, prepare for where you are going, and connect with him on a new level. These questions will be your guide for several essential conversations to have with your son now. Together, you can navigate successfully through the adolescent years and guide him toward maturity. Let's get started.

Conversation Suggestions

- Parents, start by reading the whole chapter before you start your conversation. This book is written for you; we don't expect your son to read it. His only job will be to participate in the conversation with you.

- Consider each question, as well as the perspectives offered in the chapter, and be ready to discuss your thoughts on each question with your son. Feel free to take notes, underline, or adapt the question so it is worded in a way that feels most natural to you.

- Both the parent(s) and son are invited to answer each question, but we strongly recommend you let your son answer first. Give him the gift of being a good listener. Give him time to think, listen closely to his responses, ask follow-up questions, and respect his opinions. If you judge or criticize his answers, the conversation will quickly shut down. If you really listen and care about what he's saying, you're earning the right to be heard when it is your turn to answer. These are not questions that require quick or immediate decisions. For the most part, they are thought-provoking conversation starters.

"How Are You Feeling About These Upcoming Teen Years?"

We asked kids and parents how they felt about the upcoming teens years. Below are some of their responses:

I don't want to be a teenager because I don't want to grow up. Their schedules are packed and they can't play as many sports because it gets so competitive. Teenagers seem lazy and do not have as much energy as I do. And being ten seems more fun than being a teenager.

—Josh, age 10

I hope that as a teen, my son will have grounded Christian values and solid character, because adolescence can be tough. I'm excited for the time we have together because I can see our interest becoming more and more in line. I'm nervous for cultural influences and peer pressure that can lead teenagers astray (sex, alcohol, turning away from faith, and so on).

—Jason, father of a 13-year-old daughter and 10-year-old son

I feel both hopeful and anxious. Hopeful that my son will lean into his faith and his strengths as he becomes a more independent thinker and decision-maker. Anxious about the possibility that his weaknesses and negative peer influences could have a stronger influence.

—Jane, mom of a 13-year-old daughter and 11-year-old son

I feel anxious about protecting him from exposure to sexual images and videos online way before he can process or handle that on his own, and the long-term effects of seeing those things. I am optimistic that the challenges he faces will shape his character for the better. And I am grateful to see the seeds of faith already growing in him.

—Kelly, mom of a 13-year-old daughter and 10-year-old son

From the Parental Perspective

If you have wondered or worried about some of these same thoughts, you're not alone! Parents often feel the stress of the teenage years coming and are not sure how to respond. We love our kids and don't want them to face the same difficult experiences we encountered in our own tween to teen transitions.

One extreme is for parents to close their eyes and just hope for the best. The other extreme is to hold on so tightly in an effort to control their son that he has no other option but to rebel!

One thing is sure: There is a predictable tension between parents and their tween sons. Friends of ours compared their experience of raising four children to mountain climbing. Your

ARP Adage

As we examined our own parenting and that of our friends, we noticed three different styles of parenting. Actually, we can compare parenting styles with the way we nurture plants. Consider the following three profiles.

The Smotherer

The smotherer wants to stay in control and help the adolescent avoid mistakes.

Because of her fear, Erica shows a lack of trust and gives the impression that she is always trying to keep her son in the hothouse—holding him back as her son surges ahead toward independence. Just as plants that are kept in the hothouse too long become weak and root-bound, adolescents who are smothered may be unsure of themselves and unable to resist peer pressure. The teen who is held back may resent and reject his parents and their ideas.

The Pusher

An equally disastrous approach is to push your children out of the hothouse too soon, before they are strong enough to survive on their own.

son's job is to pull on the rope as he moves farther up the mountain, exploring and pushing himself. As parents, your job is to encourage your child as you decide how quickly you can safely let out more rope. Climbers have a technique called "belaying," which exerts friction on the rope attached to the climber so they don't fall too far should they lose their grip. Just like belaying, there is healthy tension between parents and their teenager. When each are doing their job, it will result in some necessary friction. Rather than trying to figure out *why* there is tension, wise parents accept it and recognize it as something normal and needed.

Mike is a pusher. He expects his son, John, to become an adult overnight and gives freedom too quickly. His son doesn't have the maturity to consistently make wise choices and can easily become a peer-pressure victim. Where is the balance between being a smotherer and a pusher? Consider one other option.

The Releaser

Young seedlings must be acclimatized gradually to the new environment in which they will grow by allowing them short times in the sun and wind with temperature variations in the real world outside the greenhouse. They must have a "hardening off" period. If the tender young plants aren't given this period to adjust, many will wither and die. However, if they are properly trained for survival in the new environment in which they are to grow, they will thrive.

Children also need a "hardening off" period, which gives them limited freedom and increased responsibility for themselves and their behavior under the watchful direction of their parents. Wise parents release them gradually. Your interaction with each other, which is greatly influenced by your parenting style and different personalities, will provide a foundation for helping your future teen enter the outside world.

"What Is Your Goal?"

Parenting with your goals in mind will help you navigate the teen years. After all, you wouldn't typically head out in your car without having a destination in mind. Likewise, you want to know where you are heading as a parent. The road may have twists, turns, or detours you aren't expecting, but at least you have a sense of where you are going.

A common assumption suggests the primary goal of parenting is to raise independent and well-functioning adults. However, this goal seems to be taking longer and longer today, as more and more adult children are living with their parents after high school and college. According to a Pew Research finding, 32 percent of eighteen- to thirty-four-year-olds are still living with their parents.[1] There are several economic and cultural factors contributing to the rising age for launching children; however, without clear goals around independence, it will be even easier for your son to move back into your home, where the laundry is done, the refrigerator is stocked, and the Wi-Fi is free.

To this day, I (Heather) remember the conversation my parents had with me about becoming an independent adult. They clearly communicated that after four years of college, degree or not, I would be on my own. I would be responsible for obtaining my own car and place to live. This meant I would need

ARP *Adage*

The challenge is to help him leave prepared to face life as an adult and also with a positive relationship with you! So take the time now to set goals and come up with your plan of release.

to have a job and a plan upon college graduation. Talk about motivation! I did not feel rejected or pushed out by my parents, but instead empowered, challenged, and motivated to be independent and successful.

While independence is an important goal, it cannot come at the cost of the relationship between parent and son. Be intentional about building and maintaining a strong relationship with your tween. David and Claudia Arp suggest the relationship with your adolescent is the key factor for successfully navigating the adolescent years. But it's extremely hard to develop that relationship during the teen years if you haven't worked on it previously. Build relationship with your children early. Do it now. Don't wait until later.

Peter started building his relationship with our son during the elementary years by taking him fishing or camping and doing activities they both enjoy together. He helped coach AJ's baseball team even though he wasn't passionate about baseball himself.

I (Heather) remember how most nights our tweens would still let me tuck them in bed and pray together. This was often the time when they were willing to open up about their day, ask questions for tomorrow, and let down their guard, allowing for increased connection. I'll never forget the first time I asked my son, "What would you like me to pray for you?" The answer revealed struggles I'm sure he would have not otherwise shared. Try asking this question and see what you learn about how you can pray for your son tonight!

In addition to having a great relationship with your adult son, what other goals are important to you? What are your goals for your son spiritually, academically, relationally, physically, or financially? We want to help you think through these areas in the upcoming chapters as you develop your own plan.

How Do You See Your Son?

Perhaps you've heard of confirmation bias: the tendency to interpret new evidence as confirmation of one's existing beliefs or theories. With confirmation bias, people see what they believe and tend to ignore any evidence that contradicts that belief. In other words, if you believe the teen years are going to be a major battle with an angry, disobedient delinquent, you'll find evidence to confirm these beliefs.

As you approach the teen years, one of the most important choices you make is how you see and think about your son. Ephesians 2:10 gives us a great reminder: "For we are God's handiwork, created in Christ Jesus to do good works, which God prepared in advance for us to do." Before a painting is finished, it is often unclear what the artist is creating. When you choose to look at your son as a masterpiece under construction, you will find evidence of this truth. Your son will not be perfect. He will make mistakes. He is learning. He is being transformed. The mistakes do not define him. They are not who he is or who he will be. He is under construction. And you are working along with God to help your son discover who God created him to be and become—to do the good works God has already prepared ahead of time for him.

Choosing this mind-set will free you from getting stuck in fear and negative thinking. It will also give your son the gift of

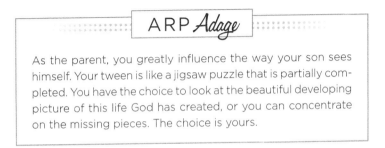

ARP *Adage*

As the parent, you greatly influence the way your son sees himself. Your tween is like a jigsaw puzzle that is partially completed. You have the choice to look at the beautiful developing picture of this life God has created, or you can concentrate on the missing pieces. The choice is yours.

someone believing in him and continually pointing him back to truth. It is so easy to listen to the pressures during the teen years. There is pressure for parents and teens alike. The good news is, God's got this! He's got plans for your son. Your job is to help your son continue to seek God and His plans. It's not your job to create a perfect man. You can't. Let go of this unrealistic expectation and rest in the truth that God is at work in your son's life.

Implementing some practical activities to remember this mind-set will help you throughout the teen years. Consider trying one of the following.

Make a Prayer Diary

In a notebook, list general things you are praying for your child. On page two start a running diary of prayer requests. You do not have to write something every day. You will know when you feel the need to add an entry—when you are about to start nagging! Allow plenty of space to write in the answered prayer later. We have kept prayer diaries for many years. Now it's rewarding to read back through them and see just how faithful God is. This activity will encourage you for many years to come. (We suggest using a real paper notebook, as digital files can easily be misplaced or deleted. Real paper notebooks tend to stick around.)

Make a Positive Log Notebook

Using a small notebook, on the first page write your own description of your son's unique personality. On the next page, begin a running diary of positive things you observe about your tween. Date each entry. You don't have to write something in your notebook each day or even each week, but whenever you observe something special about him or something really positive, record it. On the days you are ready to resign as resident parent, pull out your Positive Log Notebook and note that tomorrow will probably be better than today. It will help you keep your perspective.

"What Should the Majors and Minors Be?"

Too often we tend to major on the minors. Having a clear sense of your parenting goals will help you identify the "majors" on which you will hold firm and the "minors" you can easily let go. Try asking your son today, "What are the things we as parents major on?" You may be surprised by an answer like this: "Always have a clean room, be on time, and brush my teeth and hair." Really?

If a goal is to focus on your son's character—respect, honesty, independence, hard work, strength in the face of peer pressure—how much time are you majoring on these things? It's easy for a teen to believe the majors are video games, clean rooms, less junk food, and homework, when a parent spends the majority of conversation and energy on these topics. Through years of experience, the Arps have become experts on this topic of majors and minors.

Several years ago, we (the Arps) were the keynote speakers at a weeklong family conference. Most of our keynote addresses

ARP *Adage*

You are not looking at a finished puzzle picture! And you are not producing people—you are working with God to facilitate a precious life. Seek to understand and accept that unique child God has loaned to you for a while. In the future, your love and acceptance can translate into a caring and close relationship.

ARP *Adage*

We need to decide on the majors because you simply cannot major in everything! Ask yourself this question: "Do the major issues coincide with what I am saying to my children every day, or am I majoring on the minors?"

were to the parents; however, on this evening the teenagers were also part of our audience. But from the expressions on their faces, we could sense that they would rather be anywhere else!

First, we thanked the teenagers for dragging their parents to this meeting despite their uncooperative attitudes. A few chuckles encouraged us to continue. Then we introduced the topic of majors and minors. "What are the things your parents major on?" we asked. Before we knew it, we had a long list going that included everything from writing thank-you notes to eating breakfast.

Then we asked the parents what things their teenagers considered majors. It was obvious these parents and teenagers didn't live on the same planet! No wonder they seemed at cross-purposes.

Next we did something that at the time seemed risky. We asked individual families to dialogue together on what should be the majors and minors in their home and to do some negotiating. But before deciding if an issue was a major or minor, we encouraged them to ask two questions:

1. Is it a moral issue?

2. What difference will it make in light of eternity? Or even ten years?

Amazingly, as we looked around the room, parents and teens were actually talking with each other! Later, several parents told us this evening was the highlight of the whole week. Years later we continued to get good feedback. Some of the families got on the same page for the first time as to what their majors and minors should be. Such cooperation in families with adolescents usually doesn't happen spontaneously.

Asking yourself "What battles do I want to pick?" is another way to identify the majors and minors. Some topics to consider putting in the minor list may be clean rooms or hairstyle. You may want to save your ammunition for the more important battles to come. Wise friends of ours, Jim and Suzette Brawner, raised three amazing kids, so we were naturally excited to hear their thoughts on parenting as we were just starting our family. They told us about this idea of picking your battles. They identified three "majors" as they determined the battles they were willing to pick. When their child made a request, they would ask themselves, "Is this dangerous, immoral, or illegal?" If not, they would often give their child the go-ahead. Filtering through these three criteria made it easy to know the answer if their son wanted to shave his head or spend his money on some crazy gadget. Since it wasn't dangerous, illegal, or immoral, the answer would be yes. Their son never did ask to shave his hair, but their answer was ready.

Another helpful question to ask is "What difference will this make in the light of eternity?" This powerful question brings great perspective. Your son does not need you nagging him over minor issues. Trusting God with his life—withstanding peer pressure, developing a positive attitude, and learning good decision-making skills—are the more important issues that will serve him throughout life.

Let us say it one more time: Major on the majors and minor on the minors. Some battles with adolescents are not worth waging war—plus, you will lose the war. Psychologist Dr. James Dobson was asked why, when discussing adolescents, he focuses his comments on parents instead of on adolescents. He responded that when a teenager is about to go over the falls and he is intensely angry at home and is being influenced by a carload of crummy friends, it's the parent who can make the difference. In his newspaper column, Dr. Dobson cautions parents about being idealistic and perfectionists. It's easy to rock the boat. He writes, "Be very careful with him. Pick and choose what is worth fighting for, and settle for something less than perfection on issues that don't really matter." Dr. Dobson's good advice says, "Just get him through it!"[2]

After examining my own questions and conversations each morning with my kids, I (Heather) began to make some subtle changes. Instead of asking the same questions each morning: "Did you brush your teeth? Did you make your bed?" and so on, I began adding questions and conversations with bigger-picture goals. I would play praise music and talk with the kids about what I was reading and learning through my time in the Bible. I would ask the kids, "What did you read in your devotion this morning?" My hope is the kids will learn and enjoy the importance of starting each day with God and make it a lifelong habit.

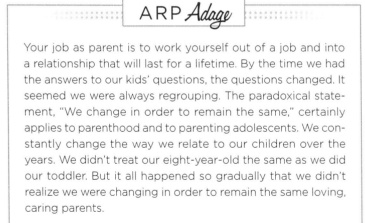

ARP *Adage*

Your job as parent is to work yourself out of a job and into a relationship that will last for a lifetime. By the time we had the answers to our kids' questions, the questions changed. It seemed we were always regrouping. The paradoxical statement, "We change in order to remain the same," certainly applies to parenthood and to parenting adolescents. We constantly change the way we relate to our children over the years. We didn't treat our eight-year-old the same as we did our toddler. But it all happened so gradually that we didn't realize we were changing in order to remain the same loving, caring parents.

"How Should Our Roles, as Parent and Child, Begin to Adjust as We Age? (What Is My Role?)"

Each developmental stage requires different skills or roles as parents. Here are some ways to think about common parenting stages and the roles parents can play in each season of development.

Age 0–2

Parent as constant caregiver: When your son was born, he came into the world completely dependent on you as his parent to care for his every need. He was essentially helpless. It is a parent's job to feed, bathe, and help him survive. These are the hands-on days of parenting that require twenty-four-hour vigilance. By age one they are mobile but basically have no judgment! Remember the days of baby gates and safety latches? He depends on you to keep him safe and meet his every need. Care for him spiritually in these days as well by lifting him up in prayer. Many parents start praying for their child before they are even born or conceived. Do not underestimate the power of praying for your son. Prayer is key for you, your marriage, and your child to thrive.

Age 2–12

Parent as teacher: As the baby boy grows and begins to toddle around, it is a parent's job to teach. Teaching how to do basic things such as feeding himself, walking, potty training, and brushing his teeth to name just a few. Parents also begin teaching acceptable ways to talk, respond when given things, ask for things, and play with others. Remember teaching him to throw a ball, swim, or ride his bike? These are important milestones in his life. As your son grows and heads off to school, he will have more experiences with other teachers, coaches, and instructors.

Through the elementary and tween years, your teaching role continues as you equip him to handle simple chores, make choices in getting dressed, or decide what activities to try. Parents have an opportunity to teach family values and spiritual truths during these years. As your son is exposed to more and more instruction from others, you have the chance to talk about how to respond with grace when someone believes something you and your family do not hold to be true. Maybe your tween will start asking new kinds of questions about why you believe what you believe. Be honest and open to his questions. It will help you as you move into the next parenting role: parenting teenagers.

Age 13–18

Coach: When we are talking about a coach here, think "life coach" as opposed to sports coach. A life coach comes alongside others and encourages, challenges, and guides them. One powerful tool for a parent-coach is asking open-ended questions, allowing their son to consider for himself what makes a good decision, allowing him to weigh his options.

As a coach, try answering a question with a question: "Well, what do you think of that?" or "What do you think is the best thing to do in this situation?" or "What are your options?" It's easy to give instant answers, so as parents we have to check ourselves before we offer advice.

Coaching requires less talking, teaching, or "lecturing" as perceived by teens. Instead, there is more listening. A good coach will help uphold a goal for their son so when he is feeling discouraged or like "it's too hard," he has someone to remind him of who he is, where he is going, and all he has to help

ARP *Adage*

Sometimes you need to simply listen to your children and save your advice for the family dog!

ARP *Adage*

Before speaking, ask yourself, *Will what I'm about to say build up and encourage my child to grow as a person, or will it attack and tear down my child?* "A gentle answer turns away wrath, but a harsh word stirs up anger" (Proverbs 15:1).

him get there. The teaching from previous years will help him remember these foundational truths.

Age 18 and Up

Consultant: As parents, your job is not over. The role of consultant is still important but requires less daily energy from you. A consultant is someone who your son may choose to call upon or not. Just like a consultant, he may choose to take your advice or leave it. There is no need to assert your way over his; no need for manipulation or guilt. In fact, the more measured and balanced you are in offering your opinions, the more likely he will be to seek and respect your consultation. He is now an adult and should be prepared to go through his own decision-making process.

Remember, prayer is important in every stage of parenting. Ephesians 1:16–18 says it well:

> I have not stopped giving thanks for you, remembering you in my prayers. I keep asking that the God of our Lord Jesus Christ, the glorious Father, may give you the Spirit of wisdom and revelation, so that you may know him better. I pray that the eyes of your heart may be enlightened in order that you may know the hope to which he has called you, the riches of his glorious inheritance in his holy people.

Adjusting our roles as parents can be subtle but necessary. Take for example one mom's experience of shifting her role. As a former teacher, Amy knew the importance of being firm yet loving with her kids. When her three children were in the toddler and elementary years, she knew how to direct and instruct them. Her punishment was always firm and fair. There was no room for these kids to talk back or have a fit to change her mind. This parenting style was working great for these young kids who understood the word *no* and responded with respect and obedience. As her children grew, this approach continued to work well with her oldest daughter, who was easygoing and always a compliant pleaser, but when the middle child, Cal, turned thirteen, Amy noticed this firm teaching style wasn't working as well.

Here's the story. Cal had been invited to go mountain biking with some friends. His bike had a flat tire and his parents were out on a walk, so he decided it must be okay to borrow Mom's bike for the off-road excursion. When he got home, he found his mom was not pleased he had taken the bike without permission. To make matters worse, the tire rim had been bent on the outing and was going to require a repair and perhaps a new tire.

Without any hesitation, Amy told Cal his consequence would be to pay for the tire repair. Cal wasn't too excited about this, but there was no talking back. It all seemed to be going as it had in the past: Child misbehaves, parent gives natural consequence, child accepts consequence and hopefully learns valuable lesson and doesn't repeat the misbehavior. End of story.

Well, not quite. Cal had been mowing lawns for several neighbors for an entire month in an effort to earn some extra money. He had been looking forward to taking the money and going to play paintball with his friends. On payday, Amy came to collect the money from Cal to pay for the bike repair. This is when the wheels came off!

Instead of obediently handing over the money to Amy, Cal argued and pleaded. Finally, out of frustration, Cal took off to his room and slammed the door, leaving Amy confused and frustrated. As a mom, Amy wanted her son to know she loved him, but she also needed Cal to understand the importance of taking personal responsibility for making his mistakes right. He might be learning the personal responsibility, but she could see Cal was not feeling loved at the moment. Amy realized she needed to try another approach.

After they both had some time to cool down, Amy invited Cal to sit with her on the patio. She let him know she would like to try a new method of communication where they each take turns sharing their thoughts and feelings as the listener reflects back what they hear and validates the speaker's feelings. First Cal shared. Amy listened as he explained how hard it was to have worked so hard to earn this money for a month and how frustrating it was to have to just hand it all over for a bike tire. He felt completely defeated.

Then Cal got a chance to listen as his mom explained how frustrated she was to come home from her walk and find not only her bike gone without her permission, but damaged upon return. She asked Cal if he could explain how the tire got bent. Cal had a chance to confess what had happened. He explained how he and his friends took a wrong turn while mountain biking and were stuck behind a fence. He thought he could just toss the bike over the fence and it would be okay, but it's probably when the tire got bent. It had been an accident.

Since much of Cal's frustration came from having to hand over all of the money at once, he asked Amy if it was okay to give half the money to cover the tire and then come up with a payment plan to cover the rest of the cost. This seemed like a reasonable compromise to Amy.

But the best part of the story was still unfolding. After Amy took the time to really hear and understand Cal's feelings and show him love and grace, while staying firm on her principle of responsibility, Cal shyly asked for a hug! This big thirteen-year-old wanted to be hugged and held. Cal knew he was loved. He was no longer closed off in his room in anger and frustration. Amy saw how changing her role from the teacher and instructor to the curious coach was the way to keep Cal's spirit open and help him take ownership of his behavior.

"What Is Mom's Role/Dad's Role?"

As parents, we have a unique relationship with our children. My relationship as Mom looks different from my husband's relationship as Dad. As my son grows, I want him to learn to become a godly man, husband, and father. He needs to be watching and learning more from his dad during these years. This may require an intentional shift in my relationship with him.

For me the shift is not about pulling away from our son, but redirecting his questions and concerns to his dad. I want my son to still feel safe to ask tough questions or tell me what is going on for him. In those moments, I want to ask him questions about what he thinks and what he knows and be willing to share my thoughts. A new emphasis, however, has been to encourage him to talk with Peter about these things as well—pointing out that his dad may have more to offer on the subject since he's a man. I wasn't as conscious of this when AJ was young, but as he grows I want him to seek godly men for advice, not just his mom.

Moms also need to allow space for their sons to really bond with their father figures, have some adventures, and do some things that may be out of a mom's comfort zone. This is an important part of your boy's journey. For example, Peter took AJ on camping trips, fishing and hunting excursions, skiing adventures, and even to monster truck rallies. Just as it is crucial for moms to comfort and nurture their boys as small children, it is important to release your son from Mom's protection and let him be pushed, challenged, and encouraged to share new experiences with Dad.

One dad, Chris, told us why he is being so intentional with his three sons these days. He talked about how marketers are being intentional. They are paying attention to everything our boys do online or on their smartphones. They know their age and where they live and want to strategically introduce them to all sorts of things and influence their behavior, especially their buying priorities. Chris pointed out that if marketing companies are being that intentional, we also need to be intentional as parents. He actually tries to do his research on his sons, paying attention to what they like and their gifts and their passions. He tries to connect with them on that level to spend time, build relationships, and provide guidance. Dads can be great role models and must not relinquish their crucial role to the corporate or pop-culture world. Somebody or something is going to influence your son today. Make sure your voice is part of the message he receives.

If you are a single mom, we encourage you to help your son develop relationships with mature, godly men. You may find these men in your church, a youth leader, or other community program. You may even encourage a strong relationship with a godly grandfather or uncle. As boys grow, they want and need strong male role models in their lives.

ARP *Adage*

With the high rate of divorce, too many boys are growing up without a strong male model. So how can you connect with your tween son? Any way you can! Researchers report that during these years the most important protection against developing negative patterns such as smoking, drinking, and even suicide attempts, is having a strong parental bond. A child's self-perception is greatly influenced by how they think their parents see them. So spend time building your relationship with your son! It may well be his "life insurance"!

You are ready now for your conversation with your son. Remember, you'll want to share your thoughts and hear your son's ideas about the following questions. These are questions your son may not have thought of before. It will be helpful for you to share your thoughts and excitement for these next years with him so he can start thinking about the transition from tween to teen as something positive too. A conversation is both of you talking. Ask questions. Share your answers to the questions and listen to his ideas. No one enjoys a lecture!

1. "How are you feeling about these upcoming teen years? Be honest." You want your son to be able to share honestly how he is feeling. You may want to share the qualities and attributes you see in him that will help him navigate these upcoming years.

2. "What is your goal?" Share your hopes for your son and ask him to share his dreams too. He may not have thought much about these years. Encourage him to dream about them.

3. "What should the majors and minors be?" Ask your son what he thinks are the majors and minors in your family. Take this opportunity to share your goals and ways you could together let go of more of the minors and focus on the majors.

4. "How should our roles, as parent and child, adjust as you age?" This may be a tricky question for your son to answer. Start by sharing your role of shifting from being the teacher to the coach—wanting to start thinking things through together, empowering him to have some input rather than always be the lone parental authority.

Conversation 2

• • •

THE FRIENDS TALK

The Family to Friends Shift

After a busy season of ski activity and travel, I (Heather) was excited to see a weekend on the calendar without any commitments for any of us. Looking forward to having a fun family weekend, I decided to ask each of the kids what they would most like to do for a family weekend. The girls suggested a family game night or another family favorite: making homemade egg rolls. When I asked AJ what he wanted to do for a family night, he quickly responded, "Have a sleepover at Max's" (and he did not intend to have the family join him either). My quick response—"When did you become such a teenager?"—brought a smile to both of us.

The picture is clear: Tween boys are increasingly more interested in friendships and less interested in their parents and family. Suddenly, friends' opinions become the absolute authority, even if it is coming from a thirteen-year-old. Friends will have growing influence on your son as he ages. This rising importance of friends in his life is natural and to be expected, even if it is confusing and frustrating at times. This influence is not necessarily bad or evil; it is simply a normal part of development as teens begin to crave more space and autonomy from their family.

Psychologist Lisa Damour used a swimming metaphor to explain raising teenagers. The parent is the safe side of the pool, a source of stability and sure foundation. The teenager's job is to learn to swim in the deep end on his own. When the water gets too deep, however, the teen may cling to the parent, looking for assurance, comfort, and direction. These times can be full of surprising conversation and reconnection that may not have been experienced for some time. Gone are the one-word answers and cold shoulder. Parents are excited to feel reconnected with the once-distant teen.

However, when the teen feels ready to swim again, he pushes off hard, wanting to get far away from the edge of the pool where he may be perceived as a "baby" by the other swimmers. The push can be confusing and hurtful to the parent who has just experienced a close, connected moment. Understanding that the push back into the pool isn't personal or against the parent as much as a pushing toward independence and adulthood can help during these often confusing transitional years.[1]

"What Does It Mean to Be a [fill in last name] Man?"

In conversation 1, "The Big-Picture Talk," you identified your goals during these tween to teen years. In this process, you may have noticed you have a list of family values you would like to pass on to your son. What attributes do you value? Words like *respect*, *honesty*, *hard work*, *perseverance*, *love*, and *kindness* may come to mind. Making this list is an important start. The next step is to find out what values your son already holds and what values still need to be taught.

Our family friends, Jeff and Gail, had a great tool to identify what family values "stuck" with their boys. When their youngest son turned fourteen and was about to enter his first year of high school, Jeff took all three sons on a "men only" camping trip. Jeff asked his boys "What does it mean to be a Fray man?" The boys responded and agreed that a Fray man is a man of freedom, of grace, and a contender for purity. These were the family values that stuck!

When we asked our son, "What does it mean to be a Larson man?" he responded with the values that have stuck so far. According to AJ, a Larson man is fun, adventurous, faithful, and hardworking.

Knowing what our son sees as the attributes of a Larson man helps us see what values have stuck and what values we still want him to "catch" before he is launched into adulthood. This process of naming the family values can also become an important part of his identity formation.

The Influence of Media and Friends

Boys are inundated with messages about who they are and what they are expected to be from a variety of sources. Advertisements on TV and movies are just the beginning. Now social media has found a way to advertise to young boys through video games, YouTube videos, Instagram, Twitter, and a never-ending stream of new digital media. Boys learn what to say, which energy or sports drinks are trending, and what brands to wear in terms of clothes and shoes. Make no mistake this is big business. According to a Piper Jaffray survey, middle-class teens are able to spend 30 percent of their money on clothes, compared with adults who typically spent less than 5 percent.[2]

Often the messages communicated through advertisements are if you look or act a certain way, you will be happy and have the friends and attention you want. Other messages taught through our culture and media are more negative and destructive. Many popular men are portrayed as reckless, flippant, and simply ready to party whenever they can. Heisman Trophy winner and first-round NFL quarterback pick Johnny Manziel was so iconic in his college career they named him "Johnny Football." But in his first few years in the NFL, he seems to be known less for his on-field play and more for his partying and legal problems, including being accused of assaulting his girlfriend. To date, he's certainly not been the role model young boys need to follow. But this negative storyline is a common one for many male actors, musicians, and sports stars.

Peers make up another strong influence on our tween boys. As we've already pointed out, friends become one of the loudest voices in your son's ears during the tween years. The voices of his peers seem only to grow louder as they determine what's cool or acceptable in terms of clothes, music, relationships, humor, slang, and behavior. Since this transition is so predictable, it is both strategic and important to talk about his choices in friends before the teen years.

A friend shared this story about her twelve-year-old son. It's a classic example of peer pressure without once mentioning the words.

My son had never cared much about what he looked like. Day after day he would stumble out of bed and throw on a pair of basketball shorts and a mismatched shirt. He wouldn't even brush his hair most days before going to school. Then one day out of the blue he came downstairs wearing a button-down collared shirt and matching khaki shorts, wondering where the hair gel was because he actually wanted to style his hair. Who is this kid? And where has he been all the years I have tried to have him match and do his hair? From that moment on he dressed to impress and cared about what he looked like.

Guess you could describe this as positive peer pressure. Here are some other ways peer pressure can be positive:

Peers who share a common faith and values

Peers who are good examples (grades, sports, loyalty, and so on)

Peers who are encouraging and give positive feedback and good advice

Peers who are kind and inclusive

Friends have the power to communicate all kinds of messages, either positive or negative, to your son. These messages are communicated with words as well as nonverbal cues. It can be the way another boy ignores him, where friends choose to sit or not sit during lunch, whether they invite him to join the pickup game after school, or if they "like" his post on social media. There are so many ways to communicate, and tweens are masters at finding feedback about their value or worth from others. Unfortunately, much of the feedback is negative or misinterpreted, and hence, inflicts a lot of pain and misunderstanding! Which messages will land?

POSITIVE MESSAGES	NEGATIVE MESSAGES
You are awesome and fun to be with.	You are so uncool and not wanted.
You are smart and capable.	You are stupid. You're a geek!
You are strong and athletic.	You are weak and don't measure up.
You are kind and a good friend.	You're no fun to be around.

ARP *Adage*

Get to know his friends. The best way to encourage your son to have appropriate relationships is to stay in touch with his friendship circle. We always encouraged our sons to invite their friends to our home. We didn't worry about grass—our yard was the neighborhood soccer practice field—so we didn't have to worry about the other kind of grass, the drug kind.

Our sons are inundated with messages of who they are and what they are worth during the teen years. Tragically, they are often lies to help marketers sell something or half-truths whispered by insecure peers to make themselves feel better.

What Messages Does My Son Need From Me?

Parents have a responsibility to be the voice of truth, reminding their son who he is amongst the crazy din of media, friends, and school. What are the messages you want your son to know about himself? Make a list of them and begin to share them with him.

Some messages may include:

- You are fearfully and wonderfully made. (Psalm 139:14)
- You are a masterpiece and a new creation in Christ. (2 Corinthians 5:17)
- You are able to do all things. (Philippians 4:13)
- You are created for a purpose. (Ephesians 2:10)
- You have been set apart. (Hebrews 10:10)

In his book *You Have What It Takes*, John Eldredge encourages readers to "look at the stories boys love, the games they play. They are full of battle and adventure and danger. They love to build things . . . and then blow 'em up. They love to jump off stuff."[3]

Eldredge is challenging readers to think about how their sons are wired and what this tells us about their needs. His main premise is that every young boy, deep in his soul, wants to be a hero and be powerful and know that he has what it takes. He wants to know he measures up.

Perhaps this is why boys keep score, compete, and argue about the rules and fair teams. They constantly try to one-up each other, whether physically or verbally. They test their abilities and compare themselves to each other. Who is the tallest, fastest, or strongest? Who can jump the highest, throw the farthest, or hold their breath the longest? The competitions never end.

Practically speaking, no boy wins every competition. Inevitably your son will come home some days feeling like a loser, like he doesn't measure up. As parents, we can help impart truths that are larger than the middle school narratives, more enduring than the days' successes and failures.

Here are some practical tips for relating to your adolescent son:

- *Give unconditional love.* Adolescent boys need parents who base their love and acceptance not on their son's performance, attitude, or mood, but on grace and unconditional love. One parent told us, "My child is having a difficult time growing up, so each morning I give him a clean slate. I erase all the hurts, mistakes, and angry words spoken yesterday, and give him the gift of a fresh start."

- *Remember that this phase is temporary!* Adolescence is time-limited. While some experts now say that adolescence may extend into the early twenties, it will come to an end. One day your son will be an adult. Let that fact encourage you and provide perspective when he is difficult, careless, or forgetful in the adolescent years!

- *Concentrate on the relationship.* Our central message throughout this book is to keep building an open, honest relationship with your son. At times it will seem as if you are doing all of the work. Teenage boys can be especially distant, quiet, and rude. Tolerate what you can and do all you can to preserve the relationship. At a critical point it could well be the lifeline your son needs!

- *Be brave enough to say no.* According to Dr. Mary Pipher, research reveals the best family is the one in which the message children receive from parents is "we love you, but you must do as we say." She points out that adolescents do not deal well with ambiguity. So it's fine to establish limits.[4]

- *Give a lot of affirmation.* Help your son make the most of his best attributes—whether physical or mental—and look daily for ways to give affirmation. Encourage him to keep achieving academically, and if athletic, to remain active in sports. Encourage him to adopt healthy habits, which include a healthy balance of activity, sleep, and limited screen time. Whenever you can, give him an honest compliment. Whether you believe it or not, if he is like most adolescents, he cares deeply about what you think of him.

- *Make a positive list.* Use this verse as a guide and make your own positive list. Here is our paraphrase: "Finally, parents, whatever is true about your child, whatever is honorable, whatever is just, whatever is pure, whatever is lovely, whatever is gracious, if there is any excellence, if there is anything worthy of praise in your child's life, think about those things" (adapted from Philippians 4:8).

- *Have a sense of humor.* One surefire way to get my son laughing is to poke fun at myself. I am not opposed to recognizing my own idiosyncrasies and calling myself out for them, and they frequently make my son chuckle (in a good way, not in a "see, I knew you were dumb!" kind of way). Nothing sets a tween in a sourer mood than being with parents who are super uptight!

"How Would You Want Others to Describe You?"

Stop now and answer this question for yourself as a parent. Did you list what you do, your job, or the roles you fill? Did you describe your personality or character qualities? We are each unique individuals who bring certain defining qualities with us. Other attributes are being refined in us through the power of the Holy Spirit, time, and maturity. Let's look at a theory on personality and some thoughts about character and attitude.

Personality

Since your son's birth, you have seen his personality unfold. Maybe you were able to identify some of his personality and temperament even in the womb. Babies quickly reveal their temperament by the way they eat, sleep, interact, and play.

There are many theories around temperament and personality, and discovering your son's natural tendencies can be helpful during these tween years. Be careful, though: Many psychologists agree that personality is still being formed until around the age

ARP *Adage*

Humor was often a lifesaver in our home. We remember a very intense conversation with one of our sons when he suddenly looked up to heaven and said, "Humor, where are you when I need you?" That broke the tension and we all laughed. To this day we remember laughing but couldn't tell you what serious issue we were discussing.

of thirty. Putting labels on your child can limit them or box them into being someone they are not.

One leading personality model known as the "Big Five" separates personality into five components including openness to experience, conscientiousness, extroversion, agreeableness, and emotionality. These components are generally stable over time and appear to be attributable to a person's genetics rather than the effects of one's environment.[5]

Interestingly, these five personality factors appear to be consistent across cultures as well. Take a moment to think about where your son falls on these continuums.

1. Openness to Experience:

    Conventional .... Progressive, Adventurous

2. Conscientiousness:

    Disorganized .... Organized and Goal-Oriented

3. Extroversion:

    Introverted, Shy .... Extroverted, Social

4. Agreeableness:

    Competitive, Assertive .... Pleasing, Agreeable

5. Emotionality:

    Less Expressive, Calm .... Highly Emotional, Reactive

Studying our kids' personalities encourages us to concentrate on their strengths and, at the same time, help them overcome their weaknesses. It also helps us as parents to manage our own expectations. Remember, God made your child to be a unique individual, not a clone of you!

Next analyze yourself using the same grid. After all, you're part of this equation. So is your spouse. Where do you fall on these continuums? Take some time and reflect on how the personality mix in your home contributes to parenting/relational outcomes.

Merton and Irene Strommen (he is a noted research psychologist; she is a former public school teacher) said in their book *Five Cries of Parents*:

> Poor parenting can result from a parent's unresolved personal problems. There are brilliant psychiatrists and psychologists who know a great deal about the human personality, but are inept as parents. Their insecurities and needs, obvious to others but not to themselves, profoundly influence their actions. Though insightful and effective when helping others, they lose their effectiveness when dealing with issues that touch their own lives. Having observed this phenomenon again and again, we find it crucial to encourage all parents to reflect on themselves as people and as a couple, as well as parents.[6]

Your personality will affect how you relate to your adolescent. Assess your own temperament and be as alert to your own tendencies as you are to your child's. Do what you can to understand your son and yourself, but remember to be flexible and open to changes up ahead.

Character and Attitude

Attitude is something you can choose each day. Attitude is defined as a settled way of thinking or feeling about someone or

ARP *Adage*

The trouble with figuring out what our kids are like is that by the time we do, they've done another flip-flop. The only thing that you can count on during adolescence is change!

something. The thoughts or feelings are then typically reflected in a person's behavior, especially toward others.

Let's take mornings in our home (the Larsons). Our son has never been a morning person. He would rather sleep late, and even if he's up early, he does not want to eat or talk until after nine o'clock. Even though he isn't a morning person, getting up and going early is a necessity many mornings. These early mornings we've challenged him to choose his attitude and behave accordingly. He may not greet each family member with a cheerful smile, but he can still decide to be kind and gracious in his attitude toward others.

Character is also a choice. The moral decisions people make reflect their character. When thinking about character, attributes such as honesty, integrity, courage, respect, responsibility, diligence, and compassion come to mind.

If respect is important in your family, how do you treat others with respect? What do you need to do differently to model respect? Think through what respect looks like and feels like. Who is it important to treat with respect: family, friends, teachers, pastors, strangers, clerks, homeless people? Recently an adult friend asked us how to treat a brother who is choosing an affair over his family, which brings up the question: How do you treat someone with respect if they are not making choices or decisions you respect?

When I (Peter) was in practice as a therapist, I was working with a mother and her twelve-year-old son concerning some behavioral issues he was exhibiting at home and school. One of the recurring themes she kept bringing up was how she wanted him to respect her. As we unpacked some of their relationship patterns, it became clear that she often said and did things she later regretted, having lost her temper and becoming highly reactive to difficult situations. When complaining about wanting respect, she was very struck by the insight, "If I want to be respected, I need to behave in a more respectable way myself."

ARP *Adage*

Our sons had a strong sense of justice and would call our hand on any inconsistencies, however small. One day our oldest and very verbal son commented, "The problem with being a teenager is your jury is also your judge." (He's now an attorney. ☺)

Think about the fruits of the Spirit Paul describes in Galatians 5:22. These "fruits" are attributes God develops in people, and they are also attitudes or character qualities a person can display. A person can choose to be loving, joyful, peaceful, patient, kind, good, faithful, gentle, and self-controlled. Obviously, in our own strength, we all fall short of this list, but with the Holy Spirit these attitudes and character traits can develop in us over time. As parents, we have a responsibility to not only teach these attitudes and character traits, but to also model them for our children.

"Who Will You Hang Around With to Help You Be the Person You Want to Be? How Do You Choose a Good Friend?"

Often, boys are just discovering who they are during the teen years. Their personality may be developing, and they are making daily choices about their attitude and character, but they are still discovering their identity.

As adults, we can more readily identify who we are and what we like. Knowing these pieces helps us discern who will make a good friend. For instance, I (Heather) am a mom, a wife, a coach, and a friend who enjoys cooking, running, and being outdoors. I'm a positive person who enjoys encouraging others and being around other women who love God and aren't afraid to have fun.

ARP *Adage*

Even though you can't choose your son's friends for him, you can help create an environment in your home where he feels safe and loved. The Arp Family Motto: On our team, we build each other up—there are plenty of people out there who will tear us down!

However, when I was a teen, I wasn't sure who I was or what I liked to do, and had no well-defined criteria for identifying who would make a good friend. Recently, a tween put it this way: "If I don't know who I am, how can I find my brand?" Knowing more about who you are and who you are not helps tweens attract others who are like them and let go of friends who may be pursuing other priorities.

These friend groups may need to be flexible as tweens grow and identify more clearly who they are becoming. Stephen had been a competitive baseball player who played with an elite traveling team and coach. Baseball practice, conditioning, or preparing for the next tournament consumed his days. He began to sense he was out of balance and wanted to find a team where he could still enjoy playing the game without quite so much intensity. By changing to a house league team, he found more balance and a group of friends who also enjoyed a range of activities, including baseball. It was hard to release some of the friends who judged him for switching teams, but in the end he found his "brand."

Choosing good friends during the teen years in crucial. Friends can provide a great source of strength and accountability. Our son, AJ, recently had a chance to be very intentional about where and how he was making friends. We moved across the country the summer between his eighth grade and freshman year. As school started back up, he immediately got involved in a local church youth group, Young Life, and a weekly Bible study that meets before school. We were super impressed with the ways he continually put himself in settings where he could meet boys with similar priorities and character. Together they encourage one another in the face of temptations at school and in relationships. They have one another to talk to and ask for prayer.

Writer Josh Wiley has identified several passages in the Bible (ESV) about choosing good friends:[7]

One who is righteous is a guide to his neighbor, but the way of the wicked leads them astray.

Proverbs 12:26

Whoever walks with the wise becomes wise, but the companion of fools will suffer harm.

Proverbs 13:20

A scoffer seeks wisdom in vain, but knowledge is easy for a man of understanding. Leave the presence of a fool, for there you do not meet words of knowledge.

Proverbs 14:6–7

Make no friendship with a man given to anger, nor go with a wrathful man, lest you learn his ways and entangle yourself in a snare.

Proverbs 22:24–25

Do not be deceived: "Bad company ruins good morals."

1 Corinthians 15:33

1. "What does it mean to be a [fill in last name] man?" Let your son list the qualities he sees as important in your family. You may want to ask him about how media or friends might be sending him different messages. Tell him some of the messages you hope he will be hearing from you today and throughout the upcoming teen years.

2. "How would you want others to describe you?" Show him the personality categories and ask him to describe where he sees himself on each continuum. Let him describe where he sees you as his parent. Talk together about the strengths and challenges of each spectrum. How will your personalities relate with one another? Are you similar or different? Will these similarities or differences make things easier or more challenging? Discuss the differences between personality, character, and attitude. Ask him how he thinks others might describe his character and attitude?

3. "Who will you hang around with to help you be the person you want to be? How do you choose a good friend?" Talk together about what characteristics make a good friend. Remind your son that being a good friend will help him find good friends.

PROJECT THIRTEEN

The onset of the teen years comes with insecurities and fears for both parents and adolescent. Most tweens long for their parents to acknowledge that they are growing up and not treat them "like little kids." For good reasons, many cultures provide a rite of passage into adolescence. Your son is going through a huge developmental transition and needs reassurance and the recognition that he can make it. Providing adequate structure will help him feel safe, in control of his life, and prepared for the future. To help with that pursuit, we (the Arps) want to suggest a practical project that helped us and many other parents successfully prepare our teenagers for the world of adulthood.[1]

We call this rite of passage Project Thirteen, which is a planned one-time challenge to help your son prepare for the teen years. It has proven to be very popular with both parents and their tweens. For that reason, we want to pause the conversations and briefly present this idea for your consideration.

Project Thirteen

Julia, the mom of a twelve-year-old boy, exclaimed, "Adolescence is such a scary time to even think about letting go. Plus, I already feel like I'm losing control!"

"You *are* losing control," I (Claudia) told her. "That's what it's all about. But you want to lose control in a controlled manner!"

Today, as you look at your son, as scary as it may be, you are going to lose control whether you plan for it or not. So what can you do to get this process started on a positive note?

Fortunately, kids come programmed for independence. Their job is to break away and become autonomous people. Communicate to your son that a day is coming when he will grow up and leave your home, and a significant part of your job, as the parent, is to help facilitate this process. When he realizes you are aware that he is maturing and growing up, he might be much more cooperative.

As parents, we have the unique privilege of equipping our kids for life. There are many progressive milestones along the way. Our job is to make sure they are safe and can care for themselves, as you make sure they can swim, ride a bike, read, prepare a meal, clean up after themselves, and eventually even drive a car. This project is designed to intentionally further your child's abilities as he matures into a teenager.

So let us share with you a strategy for launching kids into the teenage years, which was shared with us years ago by our friends Paul and Phyllis Stanley. Project Thirteen will help your son enter the teen years a little less shaky, a little more self-assured, and a little more positive. And as the parent, you can embrace this new phase of family life with real hope instead of a sense of impending doom.

Designing the Project

Several months before your son's thirteenth birthday, present the idea of Project Thirteen to him and together decide what to include in the challenge. Relay to your son something like this: "We're excited that in a few months you are going to be a teenager. We are entering a new phase of family life. No longer will we relate to you as a child. Actually, you are becoming a 'pre-adult,' and we want to build a more adult relationship with you. We want to help you prepare for your teen years by giving you a one-time project that we call Project Thirteen."

Then explain the project, which includes goals in four different areas: physical, intellectual, spiritual, and practical. For motivation, tell your son, "If you complete it by your thirteenth birthday, you will receive a reward."

After explaining the concept, you could say something like, "I'd like you to think about how you would like to grow in each of these areas. Brainstorm specific projects or activities you could do in these areas. Then we'll sit down together and write the project."

Along with this proposal is an important message: "We are excited! (instead of scared and anxious). You are getting ready to enter a special time of life. You're on your way to adulthood. We want to help you be ready for this new phase of your life, and this challenge will help you prepare. It is a big deal! You are going to be a teenager, and we are happy about this!"

Positive excitement is contagious, and hopefully you can infect your son with a positive attitude of anticipation and also give the gift of advance preparation.

Be creative. Customize the challenge to fit your son's individual needs and personality. If your son has difficulty handling money, you could challenge him to learn how to keep a budget. Or maybe he needs to learn some practical skills like cooking a meal, washing and folding his own laundry, or typing on a keyboard.

Program the challenge for success by including challenges in some areas in which your son is gifted. But at the same time you want it to be a real challenge, or else it will have little meaning. Here is a sample Project Thirteen:

Mark's Project Thirteen

1. Physical Goals

   A. Run a mile in under seven minutes.

   B. Learn to play golf: Work on driving the ball, chipping, and putting.

2. Intellectual Goals

   A. Read a biography about someone you admire and give us an oral report.

   B. Read one classic novel.

3. Spiritual Goals

   A. Volunteer to serve at church for one week of vacation Bible school.

   B. Read the book of Proverbs (one chapter a day for a month). Write down a verse from each chapter and identify some helpful life principles.

4. Practical Goals

   A. Earn $50. Parents will match what you earn and save before your birthday.

   B. Plan and prepare a family dinner.

The timing can be flexible, but allowing enough time is essential. Summer is an ideal time to begin because your son may have more time in which to complete the challenge. One parent gave her son the challenge two weeks before his birthday; their house was in chaos for those fourteen days. A last-minute challenge is not recommended. Plan ahead.

When all the items have been checked off the Project Thirteen list, it's time to celebrate. Here are several suggestions:

1. Give your son a gift for a job well done. It may be a surprise, or he may have suggested it. Maybe it's a special experience, trip, or item he's been hoping for. Some kids need more motivation than others, so it's smart to tie the challenge in with a gift they really want. Whatever the gift, the message is, "Congratulations on a job well done. We are proud of you!"

2. Celebrate! Choose your new teenager's favorite menu. Include family and friends in the celebration. Make your teenager the star for that day and tell others about his accomplishments!

A Challenge With a Big Payoff

After completing Project Thirteen, Michael told his mom, "I like the fact that I really accomplished something." Another boy, Chris, commented, "In our class, only my friend Joe and I are really prepared to be teenagers!" At a time when so many kids feel insecure, you can give your son the gift of confidence through preparing for the coming teenage years. So when you reach this challenging stage of family life, turn it to your advantage by challenging your tween to get prepared for the teenage years. Both you and your tween will reap the many benefits in the years to come.

Steps for Creating Your Unique Project Thirteen

1. Explain Project Thirteen to your son, and give him a copy of the sample. Together discuss possible goals and projects. Ask your son to write down his own draft of the goals he would like to set.

2. Next, begin working on your version of his Project Thirteen. Consider your son's strengths and weaknesses. Choose

positive areas you would like to reinforce, but also list the areas that you would like to strengthen.

3. Write specific goals for these areas: physical, intellectual, spiritual, and practical.

4. Evaluate your Project Thirteen by answering these questions:

   • Is it practical? Have I added too much or too little?

   • Is it programmed for success? Will it stretch my son, yet be obtainable?

   • Is it measurable? Will my son know when the requirements have been met? Is there a reasonable time limit?

   • Are the rewards clearly defined?

5. Make a date with your son for lunch or dinner. Compare the two lists and work together to combine them. Be sure to include items from your son's list, and don't force all of your ideas on him.

6. Discuss the reward. Would he like it to be a surprise? Or is there a special gift he would particularly like?

7. Together, agree on a final draft of his Project Thirteen, including a date by which the challenges should be completed.

But You Don't Know My Son

Will your almost-thirteen welcome a Project Thirteen? Two of our preteen sons thought it was cool, but one responded, "Do I really have to do this?" We chose a reward that was really appealing and he was willing to go through the process to get it.

What if your son is not cooperative? You're thinking, *He'll roll his eyes if I even suggest this!*

Know your son. Some children like the formality of a challenge that is well defined. Others think it's corny. One parent said, "I knew if I wanted my son to cooperate I'd have to make it really low-key. With him, I never used the term *Project Thirteen*, but the summer before his thirteenth birthday, I began to give him little pieces of it." Adapt this to fit your son's personality.

What If My Son Fails?

What if the initial excitement fizzles out? Not all kids or parents are great at follow-through. Here's how to salvage a half-completed challenge:

First, list all your son has already accomplished and give affirmation. Focus on what has been completed. Admit it if his challenge was unrealistic, and simplify it. For instance, if his challenge included preparing meals for a week, modify that part of the challenge to cooking one three-course dinner for the family. Then talk together through the challenges yet to be met and modify them.

My Son Doesn't Need This

Some kids are super responsible, and a Project Thirteen might seem boring. If you have a child like this, look for another rite of passage to help celebrate the entrance into the teenage years. One mom let her son completely redecorate his room. This was a real "letting go," since Mom was an interior decorator, and her son chose a color scheme that mainly involved camouflage. What about challenging your resistant son to complete a service project or to write his autobiography or philosophy of life?

Too Much Work?

Yes, this is work. Parenting is hard work every day. But the work involved in organizing, challenging, and supervising this rite of passage is worth it. Project Thirteen sets the stage for the coming teen years. Two benefits for the parents are:

1. Establishing a positive and celebratory start to the teen years

2. Helping the family relate to and support one another as a team

The benefits for the tween include:

1. Beginning the teenage years with a sense of accomplishment

2. An increased awareness that his parents support his growing up

3. Helps to develop comradeship with his parents and a realization that they are on one team.

While Project Thirteen isn't a cure-all for the stormy teenage years, it is a tool you can use to navigate the rough waters of transition from tween to teen. So be creative and intentional with your son, but most of all, have fun and keep it positive.

Countdown to Adulthood

After a successful launch into the teen years, the countdown to adulthood begins. Project Thirteen sets the stage for the coming teen years. This rite of passage gives your son a positive start and helps you begin to let go and to relate to your adolescent in a more mature way.

The process of releasing our children begins almost the day they are born, but at this tween stage of life, you may need a different, more defined and targeted approach to releasing your child into adulthood. By completing this challenge, your son gains a sense of competence and accomplishment at a time in life typically filled with insecurities. He also begins to understand that you realize he is growing up and that you want to work together harmoniously to facilitate this process.

While statistics indicate that more and more kids are living at home into their twenties or thirties (or moving back home after college), our challenge to you is to use the upcoming teenage years to help prepare your son for adulthood come eighteen, so he can survive and thrive on his own at college or wherever life leads him. Project Thirteen captures the essence of the concepts presented throughout the book while offering practical guidance for putting them into practice. Whether you take all or just some of these ideas, we wish you the very best as you journey with your son on his transition from tween to teen to young adult!

Conversation 3

...

THE BODY TALK

Teen Brains and Physical Changes

"What's this on my face?!" James demands.

Out of the corner of her eye, Jennifer sees immediately the red beacon of puberty shining brightly on James's forehead.

"You've got some acne," Jennifer explains. "Let me take a look."

With hormones surging through your tween son, physical changes are right around the corner. Knowing some of the expected physical changes and understanding more about the teen brain will be helpful for both of you.

"What's Happening With These Hormones and These Emotions?"

Your son may be too young to have any physical signs of puberty, but it is not too early to talk about hormones and how

ARP *Adage*

The best time to prepare for the hormonal roller coaster is between the ages of eight and twelve, before the intensive changes of adolescence kick in! Remember, this is your son's roller coaster. You don't need to get on and take a ride with him. Instead, you can be the one he keeps his eyes on so he doesn't lose sight of the ground.

they affect the body and emotions. During the tween and teen years, the pituitary gland in the back of the brain produces and releases hormones to signal to the body it's time to grow. Although both girls and boys produce estrogen and testosterone, there is more estrogen produced in girls and testosterone produced in boys. Increased testosterone can cause a higher level of anger and impulsivity while estrogen may increase emotional sensitivity. Unfortunately, the pituitary gland releases these hormones in unpredictable waves rather than a predictable steady stream, as Dr. Dave Walsch points out in his book *Why Do They Act That Way? A Survival Guide to the Adolescent Brain for You and Your Teen.*[1]

Perhaps you've already experienced something like this. Anne is chatting with her fourteen-year-old son, David, as she cooks and he works on his homework at the kitchen table. They are having an enjoyable conversation about nothing significant when suddenly David's mood completely shifts. His face is taut with anger and he is suddenly short and disrespectful toward Anne.

Anne is completely caught off guard. *Where is this coming from? Why this sudden anger?*

Having recently attended Dr. Walsch's presentation on the teen brain, Anne begins to see that perhaps David has had a surge of testosterone. Because she was no longer taking David's response personally, she asked David to take a break in his room until he was able to cool down.

Later, she asked David if he knew what his anger was all about, or if perhaps he thought it was related to a surge of hormones. To both Anne and David's relief, they agreed that must be what happened since there was no other rational explanation for David's sudden irritability.

As a parent, it's important to step back and stop pushing your son in the moment to explain what is going on with his emotions. After all, he is as bewildered as you are and needs time and space to sort out his feelings. In the moment may not be the time to "solve the problem" or explain that his anger is out of place.

During these confusing years, having a basic understanding of what is taking place in the teen brain is useful for both sons and parents. It gives everyone a language to describe what is being experienced. It's also helpful to have a plan for what to do when your son feels like biting everyone's head off or is angry for no apparent reason. Invite him to spend some time alone cooling off. He may want to go for a walk or listen to some music to help him calm down. It's key for parents to let him move through the emotional wave without taking it personally or telling him that his feelings are wrong or he's bad. Remember, in the same way he can't control the unpredictable surges of hormones in his body, he won't always be able to manage the waves of emotion he's experiencing!

Although hormones associated with puberty play a leading role in the emotional fluctuations tweens experience, research shows that changes in the teen brain set the stage for classic adolescent behavior. In his book *Brainstorm: The Power and Purpose of the Teenage Brain*, professor and psychologist Daniel Siegel explains how the adolescent brain is actively changing to help teens move away from childhood toward independent adulthood. He refers to these changes as "remodeling." After age twelve, the brain is actively "pruning" or letting go of millions of neurons not used or needed. At the same time, the brain is also strengthening existing connections through a process called myelination. This remodeling is a process that can continue all the way up to age twenty-four.[2]

Emotions

During adolescence, a teen is learning to regulate emotions ranging from anger, fear, and shame to excitement and joy. These big emotions are often difficult for tweens and teens to control. It is typical to see them with big emotions and big reactions. While your son's reactions may seem out of proportion at times, his feelings are a very real part of his experience. Our culture often minimizes feelings, especially for boys, but helping your son see feelings as both mentionable and manageable will influence him to accept his feelings as valuable and not something to be stuffed or ignored. Feelings are a great source of information and feedback, signaling us when things are going well or not so well. Ignoring them can be damaging to the individual and those around them. If you hit your thumb with a hammer, you wouldn't ignore the pain. The pain is a signal to do something different to avoid more damage to your thumb. Thank goodness for pain! It tells us something needs to change. Stuffing or ignoring feelings and emotions can be just as unhealthy as ignoring physical pain.

Motivation

Motivation is also impacted by the changes in the adolescence brain. You will quickly notice that the things that motivated your son in elementary school may no longer motivate him in his teens. The brain development prompts him to ask himself, *Should I bother doing this? Is it worth it?* Your son's internal motivation will need to increase as external motivations begin to lose much of their value to him. In other words, he will need to find his own good reasons to care about things.

One stressed-out mom complained, "My son, Jack, doesn't care! He doesn't do his homework. His test scores are off the chart, but he doesn't even want to try in school. He isn't motivated by any consequences or rewards we seem to put in place!" Brain research shows this is because an important part of his brain associated with motivation, the limbic system, is undergoing that massive remodeling we discussed earlier. Transitioning from external to internal motivation is part of maturation during the adolescent years.

Evaluation

A necessary part of the adolescent journey involves identifying and developing one's passions. From a brain-science perspective, this process is called *evaluation*. Evaluation essentially means just what it sounds like: weighing things out and determining their value. Good teachers understand they must tap into this reality and attempt to help students arrive at the conclusion that it is worth tuning in to what they are teaching. Evaluation is when the mind asks, "Do I want to pay attention to this?" You will see your teenage son beginning to narrow his areas of interests and let go of certain activities in which he used to participate. You may see him start to specialize in one or two sports instead of being part of everything. You'll see his passion for certain activities spike, while former hobbies and interests just seem to fade away. Similar to adults, teens will evaluate opportunities and focus on the things they find most meaningful.

During elementary and middle school, Tommy had proven to be an excellent baseball player. His coaches had taken note of his catching skills and even encouraged him to receive extra training. His parents, seeing his talent, invested time and money to help him develop as a ball player. When Tommy reached high school, however, he was exposed to a number of new athletic opportunities. It was at this point he discovered his school offered an Ultimate Frisbee program, which Tommy was excited to pursue. Although he was talented at baseball, he wasn't passionate about it. When batting practice was scheduled, Tommy obediently participated, but he didn't initiate playing ball on his own. When he started playing Ultimate, he loved it! He sought out his friends on the team, practiced whenever he could, and organized pickup Ultimate games with his friends. Tommy's parents (and baseball coaches) had to come to terms with the fact that this kid was evaluating his options and choosing a new direction.

As parents, we have an opportunity to expose our teen sons to a number of experiences and grant them the freedom to evaluate and begin making their own decisions. It is their responsibility to decide if they will find something meaningful. Don't make the mistake of forcing them to embrace your interests. This often leads to resistance and resentment down the road. Pay attention as your son explores, and when you see him leaning into something, consider how you can support it. This is what Mark's parents did.

During his teen years, Mark found a guitar at his friend's house. He picked it up and began to learn a few chords. By the time he learned his first song, he was hooked. His interest grew and he asked his parents if he could get a guitar of his own. Despite the cost of a new guitar, his parents could tell he was really passionate about music, and they felt it was much better than sitting around playing video games. Mark didn't want to take formal lessons but enjoyed spending hours with his friends discovering how to play certain songs or making up new ones. In college, he formed a band with some friends and created a lifelong hobby.

Attachment

Another aspect of adolescent brain development involves attachment. Attachment is part of how human beings are wired to depend on, or attach to, a caregiver for survival. A good example of this attachment instinct involves coping with a perceived threat. When a threat is perceived by an infant or young child, typically the brain triggers them to move toward their caregiver for protection and comfort. You have seen a shy or scared child cling to their mother. However, if the caregiver is also the one who is emitting the threatening behavior, the child is conflicted inside. The threat their brain tells them to avoid is the same person their brain is telling them to move toward. It is a true no-win situation that can disrupt normal attachment. Dr. Siegel emphasizes there is no perfect parent but also points out there is always time to make a repair if attachment has been negatively impacted.

Attachment sets the stage for relationships, helping humans learn how to engage with others. The adolescent brain is driving your son to attach to his peers. He will be expanding his relational attachments beyond just parents to include his peers. When a threat is perceived, his instinct will now be to seek the familiarity and comfort of his friends instead of his parents. This shift is both normal and healthy.

Sixteen-year-old Jordan came home from school announcing to his dad, "I have to have those new Nikes. *All* the guys are wearing them. I'm the *only* one wearing these old shoes." Finally he declared, "If I can't have them, I can't go to school. I'll just have to flunk out."

As a rational parent, his dad, Eric, could see this line of thinking was crazy. Wrong shoes do not equate to dropping out of high school. However, understanding that Jordan's brain sees the "threat" of wearing the wrong shoes as a push toward "survival" in terms of rejection versus acceptance with his peers, Eric began to understand Jordan's thinking. Instead of getting stuck in the loop of talking about the importance of education and how he can't drop out over shoes, Eric chose to empathize with Jordan about how important the shoes felt to him. Having empathy didn't require Eric to buy the shoes, just to understand how important the shoes seemed to Jordan. This type of understanding went a long way in bolstering Jordan and Eric's relationship.

As your teen grows in social engagement with others, his brain is creating new maps. He will create a stronger sense of who he is. He will be able to grow in his ability to recognize others' points of view and learn to experience empathy. As his sense of self and others develops and becomes more sophisticated, his brain will help him learn how to put the "me" and "you" together to form a healthy "we." He will learn to collaborate and work well interpersonally. But like the shoe example given above, the journey to integrating this new brain capacity can seem irrational and confusing at times.

Risk

We've all seen teens make risky or poor choices. Maybe you were one of them. I (Heather) know I was. There is a reason teen drivers are expensive to insure! As adults, it's easy to think the teen who chooses dangerous behavior just doesn't understand the risks. If they had more knowledge, they wouldn't make the dangerous choices. But research shows this isn't the case.

Most teens can identify the risks, but because of their developing brain, they are more willing and motivated to pursue novelty and danger in an experience. In other words, they may know an activity is unsafe, they just don't care because part of their developing brain craves the risk. As parents, we can equip our sons to slow down when faced with a risky decision and ask themselves, "What am I looking for here? Excitement, speed, notoriety? Is there another safer way I might find it?"

Michael loved speed. As soon as he was able to walk, it seemed he was off and running. As he grew, he loved to do everything fast. When he was young, speeding around on his bike or skateboard caused more than a few scratches and broken bones. Now Michael is sixteen with a driver's license. His love for speed has not changed. Knowing this about Michael, his parents helped him to find a racetrack where he could learn to drive a car at high speeds in a safe environment. Michael was able to meet his need for speed at the racetrack while using his self-control to keep the speed limit on public roads.

Understanding all of the changes in the adolescent brain may feel overwhelming. Remember your son is a masterpiece. He is under construction. Keep this big-picture truth in your mind as you navigate the teen years in your home. These are exciting years!

"How Do You Feel About Your Body?"

Cognitive and emotional changes aren't the only changes to be expected. As you know, your son's body will be growing and changing rapidly too. Physical changes can start as early as age eight or as late as age fifteen. This can be difficult. At an age when boys want to be big and tough, they may find themselves a head shorter than classmates or skinny and two heads taller. Instead of looking like twins on twin day at school, they look a lot more like David and Goliath.

For the teen boy, this is not funny. Often these differences can feel like a real problem. "I'm a shrimp!" one shorter tween announced next to his taller friends. In a similar way, tall boys can feel awkward about their bodies and even start to slouch or drop their head to compensate for feeling out of place. Boys will often believe "everyone else's body" is different or better. Then, just when it seems their body is finally okay, they wake up and find it still changing. Being confident in what your body looks like during these years is challenging.

Some developmental psychology research has suggested that boys and girls have very different psychological experiences when it comes to the timing of their maturation. Girls who develop early often feel mortified and don't know what to do with the extra attention this garners from their peers. While boys who develop early often have higher self-esteem related to their physical stature and maturation. It can be toughest on boys who are very late in hitting puberty, as they have to manage the feelings associated with appearing younger or weaker than their peers. Hopefully the conversation in this chapter will help your son talk about his thoughts and feelings regarding the physical transformation that's coming his way. Remind him that his body knows just what to do, and no matter what his pace of maturation will be, his value does not rest in his physical size or appearance.

Trying to fit in physically with their friends is only part of the teenager's challenge. Consider what they see in pop culture. Male movie stars, pop singers, and athletes often have "ripped" muscles, perfect bodies, flawless digitally enhanced complexions, and straight teeth with impeccable hair. When was the last time you saw a magazine with a plump and pimply teen or greasy-haired gangly-legged boy with braces featured on the cover? Um, never. Neither has your son, and he may be looking.

You may find it surprising to find the topic of eating disorders in a book for tween boys, but young men are not immune to the pressure of having a perfect body. One study found that 25 percent of people with anorexia nervosa or bulimia nervosa are male, and 36 percent of those with binge-eating disorders are male.[3] While body image is not the only thing that fuels an eating disorder, it can be a huge factor. For parents, the challenge is to teach and model healthy choices and portions without obsessing about food or body image.

Helping your son understand and accept his body starts with you. What are you modeling for him? How do you talk about your own body in front of him? Do you call yourself fat or complain about your love handles? Does he see you taking good care of your body? Are you constantly trying the latest fad diet? Do you binge-eat when you are stressed? He is watching; what is he learning?

With boys' changing bodies, it is easy to make an innocent comment, not realizing the impact of your words. "Looks like he grew out before he grew up." "He's so skinny, he'd blow over in a strong wind!" "You're still hungry? Didn't you eat dinner an hour ago?" While these comments may be made in a humorous tone, tween and teen boys can be sensitive to these remarks and start unhealthy behaviors to change their bodies. In addition to typical eating disorder behaviors including binge eating, purging, laxative abuse, and fasting for weight loss, boys may engage in steroid use, over-exercising, and over-the-counter muscle enhancers.

The teen years are full of constant changes, and many boys feel uncertain or out of control. For some, this is an age when they will use food to comfort themselves. Other boys may try to control or restrict the foods they eat in order to have a sense of power in a season of life that can feel so out of control. Schoolwork is packed with pressure and practice schedules are wearing him out! Keeping track of what and how much he eats may become one way to control at least *one* area in his life.

There are complicated cultural, social, emotional, and biological reasons some boys struggle with eating disorders. Watch for these common warning signs and get help from a therapist or eating disorder treatment center if you're concerned:

- Constant adherence to increasingly strict diets, regardless of weight
- Habitual trips to the bathroom immediately after eating
- Secretly bingeing on large amounts of food
- Hoarding large amounts of food
- Increase in consumption of laxatives, diuretics, or diet pills
- Exercising compulsively, often several hours per day[4]

You are not responsible if your son struggles with an eating disorder. It is not your fault. But if your son refuses to eat and is losing weight, act now to get help. An excellent book dealing with anorexia is *Help Your Teenager Beat an Eating Disorder* by James Lock and Daniel Le Grange.

Reminding your son his body is great just the way it is during these years is essential. Remember, he is fearfully and wonderfully made! Every teen body is changing during these years. Often a teen's body will spring up before it fills out. Encourage your son to be confident in his body, his curly hair or straight hair, his freckles or glasses. Be careful you are not modeling negative self-talk about your own appearance. You might even agree to ban the words *fat* or *ugly* from your home.

ARP *Adage*

Besides the predictable physical and emotional changes that occur in puberty, parents must also deal with the negative message today's culture sends to adolescents.

"How Do You Feel About Our Family's Eating Habits?"

What does food mean in your family? Is ice cream a reward for good grades or a win on the soccer field? Is going out for a treat a way to cheer or comfort someone when they are feeling down? Instead of seeing food as fuel, Americans often use food as a reward or consolation.

For boys, eating is often seen as a source of pride or manliness. One family with three young boys would encourage their boys to eat large portions, cheering when one had eaten two hot dogs instead of just one. The boys learned to eat more in order to earn praise and approval from their parents. With the oldest being able to outeat the younger two, he began to eat with a mission. Eating two or three hamburgers, five pieces of chicken, and several pieces of pie became a badge of honor. It is not surprising to learn he struggled with overeating and was often teased for being "fat" as a teenager. Later, he developed a serious eating disorder in an effort to manage his weight.

The flip side of this coin is the ravenous appetite a growing boy can display. It is not uncommon to hear parents talking about their sons eating them out of house and home. Growing four to six inches in one year, playing sports, and being an active adolescent can fuel a huge appetite. As they burn all those calories, their bodies are craving more. In the same way we don't need to praise overeating, we don't need to shame our sons for being hungry all the time. Keep perspective that this is a normal phase they are going through.

When our son was younger, I (Peter) enjoyed taking him out for some special Dad time. We would often default to an excursion for a treat, such as ice cream or doughnuts. It occurred to me one day that I didn't want AJ to associate all of our special bonding time with sweets. I think some treats are fine, and I like ice cream as much as the next person, but we quickly found we could play catch, go for a bike ride, take a hike, fish, or catch a movie on our special outings. This may seem like a silly distinction, but the subtle habit of always pairing quality time with treats was headed in a direction that felt out of balance.

Our culture has become obsessed with food and weight. Think about the commercials on television. In one commercial break you'll view advertisements for fast food, then weight-loss shakes, then the biggest developments in frozen breakfast waffles, and finally an advertisement for the latest exercise equipment. What are you supposed to do? Eat more? Diet? Exercise? Finding a healthy balance can be difficult, and we would suggest the pitfalls lie in the extremes.

While your son is still in your home, you have an opportunity to teach being healthy and strong. You may understand eating sugary treats or drinking soda is okay in moderation, but how do you help your son learn to apply healthy decision-making for himself without controlling the options and making the decisions for him? Next time your son asks for a sweet or treat, instead of just giving him a yes or no answer, try coaching him around the concept of making a good choice. Ask him to reflect on what he has eaten so far today, and consider how much activity he's had. If his diet has been well balanced and he's played outside or been to practice, a treat is probably not a big deal. But if he's laid around playing video games and eating junk food all day, you may need to help him arrive at a different decision. After all, soon you will not be with him when he is choosing a snack out of the vending machine or the local convenience store with his friends and his own money.

We try to talk about being strong and healthy and finding a good balance. Teaching your son to eat enough fruits and vegetables to be healthy is as important as teaching him how much ice cream to serve himself for dessert. As he learns to manage his decisions, teach him to consider a good balance between healthy foods and not-so-healthy fats and sweets. Again, someday he will face the buffet line without you and will need to make his own choices.

"What's So Important About Clothes?"

A battle between parents and teens over clothes is not a new struggle. Check out the struggle Kristen had with her thirteen-year-old son, Blake. Blake is easygoing and typically would wear whatever Kristen has bought him in the past. Most of the time, Kristen just brought home a few pieces of clothes for Blake when she was out shopping and just put them in his room. Blake had never complained or been overly interested in what Kristen brought home.

However, as Blake was getting older, he started tuning in to what other boys were wearing. He noticed his khaki shorts and collared shirt stood out next to his friends who were in athletic shorts and T-shirts. Although he wasn't opposed to wearing the preppy clothes for church or other occasions, he wanted to get more athletic-style clothes to fit in with his friends. Blake wasn't even sure how to bring up the topic with his mom. He would complain that a shirt didn't fit right or leave the shirt in the drawer still wearing its tags. Finally, Kristen brought up the conversation. She was happy to take him shopping and help him find clothes he was more comfortable wearing.

As your son gets older, he will have a stronger opinion and want a say in what he wears. Independence in dressing is important. You want your son to discern for himself what is appropriate to wear in various situations. Remember back to the discussion about what is a major and what is a minor issue. Use the following questions to think through now what is important for your son to know about making his own choices with clothes.

What Needs to Be Covered?

This seems like a silly question to talk about with boys, but look at the current trend of sagging jeans and exposing several inches of underwear. Define with your son now what needs to be covered. Is this a battle you want to take on with your son? While one parent may say, "Let him express himself however he wants," many parents would say, "Underwear is meant to be *under* something."

Who Am I Dressing for?

During the teen years, trendy clothes and the latest fashion is often a way to feel accepted or liked. It isn't enough to just have the latest shoes; they need to be the right brand too. The race to have the right clothes and latest fashion is a competition that doesn't end after junior high or high school. Boys will need to decide whom they are dressing for. Are they dressing to impress other boys so they will feel accepted? Are they dressing to catch the eye of a girl they like? Or are they dressing to express their personal style and please themselves?

The way we dress communicates many things. Think through how you make decisions about what you wear. You will choose one outfit for a funeral and quite another to go for lunch with a friend; one for working around the house and another for going on a date. What you choose to wear can reveal your mood and intentions, and sends powerful messages to those around you.

What you wear impacts the way you feel about yourself and even the way you carry yourself! When you are wearing your bathrobe and slippers you'll feel relaxed and lounge in your favorite chair with a cup of coffee. When you are wearing a formal dress or suit with stiff shoes, you will sit up straighter and feel more proper. Your son will need to learn for himself how to choose appropriate attire for upcoming occasions. Even if he's not terribly excited about dinner at Grandma's, putting on a clean pair of jeans and shirt instead of the sweats and T-shirt he was wearing earlier may help him participate more intentionally in the evening.

Physical changes are a big part of the teen years. Having conversations now while your son is young will help you navigate these upcoming transformations and decisions. Below is a list of conversation topics to discuss.

1. "What's happening with these hormones and these emotions?" Remember, giving you both a vocabulary for the emotional swings caused by hormones and brain development will make riding the teen roller coaster easier for everyone.

2. "How do you feel about your body?" Your son is great just the way God made him! This truth is easily lost in the teen years. Start reminding him today who he is in Christ.

3. "How do you feel about our family's eating habits?" Healthy concepts like *food is fuel* and *healthy choices* are best taught now!

4. "What's so important about clothes?" Questions to consider together are: Who am I dressing for? What do I want to reflect? Ask him how he feels when he is dressed up versus when he is wearing his pajamas. Clothes impact the way we feel about ourselves and communicate powerful messages to others.

Conversation 4

• • •

THE TECHNOLOGY TALK

*Rights, Responsibilities, Privileges
(and Screens)*

Welcome to the digital world—a world that is so different from the world we grew up in! We are living in a rapidly changing technological world that gets crazier and more complicated by the day. Your challenge as the parent of a tween? The better educated you are, the better you can guide your son in this on-line world. This can be a great time to help him think through the coming years and make choices now about how much time, importance, and value he will place on his digital life. Trust us, your eleven-year-old will be much more pliable and willing to be influenced now than when he is fourteen and thinks you come from an outdated planet.

Technology is here to stay. Complaining and comparing your teen's digital world to the world you grew up in won't help. Rather than avoiding technology out of fear or frustration, we want to equip you to guide your son as you experience what is here today and prepare for what will be coming tomorrow.

The story of Rachel Canning of Morristown, New Jersey, made national headlines a few years ago as she sued her parents for "financially abandoning" her at age eighteen. Her lawsuit demanded that her parents pay her college tuition, a request they were refusing. Her father had a different take on the situation and reported that she had run away from home after failing to follow simple household rules involving chores and a curfew. After a few weeks, Rachel dropped the lawsuit and returned home, but her story raises questions about rights, responsibilities, and privileges in a culture of entitlement.[1]

Many tweens and teens assume certain privileges will be their right: "When I'm sixteen I'll get a driver's license and a car." These tweens can appear to be demanding and entitled instead of grateful. Some adults also get confused about the idea of rights versus privilege and assume their son should have access to every privilege possible. The issue is further confused by a culture that says giving our kids the very best is generous and loving, with little consideration of when this generosity becomes indulgent or misguided.

Most parents agree there are some basic rights that are the responsibility of a parent to provide: food, shelter, safety, education, health care, etc. The rights on this list are actually necessary for the healthy development of your son.

It gets fuzzy, however, when your son needs a winter coat (a legitimate right) and demands the latest trendy snowboarding brand that costs $300 and is not even waterproof (a privilege). Privileges go beyond rights and involve things that are desirable but not necessary for healthy development. Privileges include things like a smartphone, a Snapchat account, or permission to drive the car. Privileges such as these can be earned. Sometimes that means your son earns the money to purchase things himself, and other times it means he demonstrates an appropriate level of responsibility to be rewarded with a new privilege. And just as privileges can be earned, they can also be lost!

Your tween has many roles in his life. He is a son, student, friend, classmate, and maybe a brother, neighbor, or teammate. With each role he has in life, there are basic responsibilities to go along with it. It is important for your son to understand the expectations associated with these different roles. As parents, we have a standard set of responsibilities we expect from our sons. We expect our tween sons to listen to us, be respectful, and help out around the house. We expect him to be a responsible, hardworking student, getting along with his teachers and other classmates, and learning grade-appropriate material. Consciously or not, we judge our tween's behavior against these expectations, and there are consequences and rewards based on whether or not he fulfills his responsibilities. If he fails to live up to the expectations, there are usually consequences. Sometimes the consequences are natural (he gets a poor grade because he did not study), and other times the consequences are imposed by parents (he's grounded or loses access to his gaming system for a week). If he meets or exceeds expectations (he makes the National Honor Society), there may be rewards or privileges granted (he gets to stay out an hour later with his friends). Like consequences, rewards can be natural or imposed.

Help your son understand that these roles and responsibilities are not something you're assigning, but rather are simple observations about how life works. It is as true for an adult as it is for a child. As adults, we have roles and an associated set of responsibilities with being a parent, spouse, employee, etc. Like our children, we experience rewards and consequences in life based on how others judge our behavior against these role-based expectations. If you do a great job at work, perhaps you get that promotion or bonus. If you are rude to others, friends keep their distance.

One important job of parenting is to be clear with your son about the basic responsibilities you expect of him in his varying roles, such as son, brother, friend, student, teammate, musician. If he is part of extracurricular activities such as sports or music lessons, define his basic responsibilities around each of these commitments. Maturity and responsibility are displayed when these basic expectations are met consistently and independently, creating room for more privileges. If these responsibilities begin to slip, natural consequences or loss of privilege will be the result.

For the remainder of the chapter we will look at questions to help you determine your stance regarding a number of technology privilege requests that typically emerge during the teen years. While these issues involve common topics (smartphones, social media, and entertainment), they can create confusion and cause challenges for parents. We don't want to dictate the right answer on each of these topics for your family, and this is not a one-size-fits-all approach. Instead, we will process two questions designed to help you discern the best approach for your son (and family).

In the context of a specific boy's story, we'll explore answers adopted by other parents for their situations. Note that the list of topics is not comprehensive, as it mainly focuses on technology questions boys are asking. There are sure to be additional topics you need to tackle on your own, but these same principles apply.

For each of the topics listed, we suggest you define your answers to two basic questions. First, "What are the responsibilities associated with this privilege?" Consider the following issues when answering this question:

- Define what responsible behavior looks like regarding this privilege. Make sure you've made the expectations both clear and reasonable.

- Make sure, as parents, you're both on the same page. Be consistent in terms of what you communicate about expected responsibilities. Don't undermine one another and thereby confuse your son.

- As you consider the increased responsibilities (and risks) associated with this privilege, make sure your son is developmentally ready to manage it. If you determine he's not ready, it is acceptable to say, "No, not yet."

The second question is "What are the consequences and rewards if this privilege is abused or used correctly?" As you answer, consider the following:

- Just like expectations, make sure the consequences and rewards are clearly communicated to your son.

- Be consistent! If you clearly communicate an expectation and associated consequence or reward, you need to follow through on what you've said. Otherwise your voice will quickly become irrelevant and your authority to lead and guide him is undermined.

- Sometimes there are natural consequences you don't need to impose. That is even better since you don't have to be the bad guy. Instead, you can empathize and support him as he encounters important lessons. Don't rescue him so quickly that he fails to learn the lesson life is teaching.

- Keep in mind the very fact that something referred to as a "privilege" means it is a reward in itself to keep exercising that privilege.

"When Do I Get a Smartphone?"

This is a burning question for many tweens. Given the number of tweens who have a phone, your son may be convinced it is a *right*, not a *privilege*. It is our opinion, however, that this falls clearly in the privilege category. Consider that you yourself probably survived your tween years without a smartphone. Your son may already own a phone, so your process may be more about how to keep this privilege moving in a positive direction.

Austin, age twelve, is the youngest of three and could not wait to get a smartphone like his older siblings. He is a typical tween, plays on a lacrosse team, but often felt out of the loop since he was not part of the group texts that floated around amongst his friends. Finally, his parents added a line to their family plan and bought him a smartphone for Christmas. Austin immediately felt more connected because he had the latest and greatest device in his pocket. He expected to text his friends many times per day, download and play games, post awesome selfies to his newly created social media accounts, and listen to music whenever he wanted. His parents, however, had a completely different set of expectations.

What are the added responsibilities associated with this privilege?

Austin's parents believe that owning a powerful and expensive piece of technology, such as a smartphone, should provide an increased level of freedom and autonomy along with the responsibility to stay in communication through phone calls and texts. As parents, they expect him to use the smartphone to keep them informed of where he is and what his plans are. They expect him to pick up when they call, and they expect him to keep track of his phone and not treat it recklessly in ways that could break it.

In order to maintain communication with Austin, his parents expect he will have his phone charged, especially when he is heading out to situations where they need to get ahold of him, such as lacrosse practices or trips to the movies with his friends. His mother and father expect him to turn the phone off during class or dinner and pay attention to what is happening around him. To help him get sleep at night, they expect him to keep his phone in a central location, outside of his bedroom, after a certain time of night. The phone should also be kept in this location during study time so he can stay focused and complete his homework.

Austin's family spent quite a bit of time together in the car. After he and his siblings each had a smartphone, his mother noticed how their family conversations went from lively to non-existent in the car. Playing games and checking social media was taking away from conversation and observation of the world around them. They decided that using the phone to communicate with someone else (text or call) was okay in the car, but no games and social media. (Obviously, once the kids become drivers, there will need to be a new set of rules around texting and calling.) This change brought balance back to their family time in the car.

Austin's parents expect he will communicate digitally with his friends in the same mature, friendly way that he does in his face-to-face communication. They will not allow him to perpetuate lies, spread gossip about others, or threaten or bully anyone. They want him to continue to be a respectable and responsible friend in the digital world, just as he is in real life. In order to maintain this healthy type of communication, they created a rule stating that they will have knowledge of his current passwords at all times. They make it clear that, as parents, they have the right to look through his past texts or social media posts to ensure that safe and respectful communication is ongoing.

Finally, Austin's parents expect him to keep his smartphone use in balance. They don't want him to disappear into his room and spend hours on end staring at his screen. They expect him to remain active and play outside. They expect him to spend the time needed to keep his grades up. In general, Austin's parents are aware of how phone use can get out of balance, and they have made it clear they will be watching for any signs that he is sacrificing other important parts of his daily life in exchange for this new privilege.

What are the consequences and rewards if the smartphone is abused or used correctly?

Remember, agreeing on the outcomes (consequences and rewards) and following through is just as important as setting clear expectations. Austin's parents have settled on the following consequences and rewards regarding the expectations for owning a smartphone.

- If the phone is broken, damaged, or lost, Austin will have to pay for the replacement or deal with the natural consequences of a cracked screen. If he takes good care of the phone, he will have the enjoyment of a well-working device.

- If he lets the phone battery die when he leaves the house, or puts it on mute and does not respond to calls or texts from his parents, he will lose the phone for one to five days, depending on the situation. If he keeps the phone well charged, answers when his parents call or text, and uses the phone to notify them of changes in his plans, they will continue to pay for his line and let him use the phone for more enjoyable activities including games and music.

- If Austin is checking his phone during family dinner, gets in trouble for using his phone during class, or sneaks it into his room at night, he will lose it for several days, depending on the situation. If, on the other hand, he keeps it at the central charging station at night, puts it on mute during dinner and school, and doesn't use it constantly in the car, he can continue to have the privilege of using the phone. His parents might even buy him that new case he wants for it.

- When Austin uses his phone for safe and respectful communication by checking in regularly with his parents, keeping up with his grandparents, and coordinating activities with his friends, he is praised and encouraged to keep it up. If his parents find he is using his phone to exclude friends (ignoring texts from friends), they'll call him out. If he is not being a good friend, there will be natural consequences from those friends, but there may need to be more imposed consequences as well, such as apologizing to others or losing his phone for a period of time.

On one occasion, Austin had just gotten his new phone and asked his mom if he could go to the nearby convenience store with his friends. Austin's mom agreed to let him go and reminded him to be home by five for dinner and an evening church service. At 5:10 Austin wasn't home, so his mother began calling (no answer) and texting, "How close are you?" No response. Another text at 5:20: "Dinner is ready, where are you?" No response. His mother tried calling again and it went directly to voice mail. She could tell Austin had turned off the phone! When Austin finally returned home at six, his mom had left for church and his dad was there to talk through the consequences of not only breaking a curfew, but also not using his cell phone as the communication device it was intended to be. Austin made some poor excuses about not picking up in front of his friends, but in the end had his phone taken away for a week as he learned the importance of responding promptly when called or texted by his parents.

When you determine that your son's behavior is responsible, you allow him to keep using the phone as needed and gladly pay the monthly bill to have him on your data, text, and cellular plan. It almost becomes a nonissue when expectations are being met. The guidelines like the ones described above will help your son embrace privileges with increasing responsibility. You can't control him, but you can maximize your influence by being clear, reasonable, and consistent.

Remember, your end goal is to have a mature and independent adult son someday, so empowering him to manage his smartphone use is an important evolution. As he shows signs of maturity, you'll want to increase his control. After all, you can't be in his college dorm room trying to influence his smartphone use.

"How Will Social Media Be Used in Our Home?"

Long gone is the world in which you came home from school and connected with friends in person or over the landline. Now a boy's social network is with him constantly on his computer, tablet, and/or his smartphone. There is no escape; it is a constant force in his life. There are ever-increasing forms of social and digital communication bombarding our teens. The Facebook of yesterday has become the Instagram and Snapchat of today. Who knows what it will be tomorrow (when you're reading this book)? Keeping up with the specific social media channels on which your son is connecting with his friends is not easy, but it is important.

Consider Nathan, who wanted to get his first smartphone at age eleven. On the bus to and from school, he would sit with his friends as they played games, texted, and posted pictures to their Instagram accounts. This was the one thing Nathan was most excited about: Instagram. He so wanted to create an account and share pictures and posts with his friends, to see how many "followers" and "likes" he could get. He was beginning to notice that the most popular kids had the most *followers* and always received the most *likes* when they posted something. (While intriguing, it can also be a little scary to see this quantified definition of popularity so clearly displayed.)

What are the added responsibilities associated with this privilege?

As Nathan made his intentions clear to his parents, they felt it was important to sit down for a discussion and clarify their expectations.

Social networks leverage the idea of connecting, following, communicating with, and "friending" other people on the network. Kids often equate a higher number of connections with some sort of status. Because of this, it is not uncommon to friend and follow anyone and everyone. Tween boys need to realize, however, the importance of connecting only with people they know. It is possible for people with bad intentions to pose as someone else in order to develop trust. Nathan's parents told him the story of a man in his forties who was pretending to be a junior high student on a social network. Once he became an online friend with these kids, he was asking them to behave inappropriately. Luckily, he was caught. But not all stories end this well. By setting the expectation of connecting only with people he knew, Nathan's parents increased his safety.

They also informed him he was never to plan on meeting someone in person that he had met online. They let him know how dangerous this can be. They took the opportunity to tell him this applied to any digital relationship, including other participants in online games or apps, and not only the social networks in which he participated.

Another responsibility associated with social media is not sharing passwords with anyone, even friends. Nathan's parents warned him about sharing his password. Some kids will log in and pretend to be posting as someone else. The friends may think this is funny or a joke, but it can be hurtful and damage relationships.

Nathan's parents expected him to use common sense when he posted things to his account. Posts should be appropriate, respectful of others, and meet the "Grandma Rule." They explained that the Grandma Rule meant that if he wouldn't be comfortable sharing it face-to-face with his grandmother, he shouldn't post it to social media.

His parents informed him that they also needed to be connected as friends on his social network. This would allow them the ability to follow his online activity and ensure his safety. (Nathan's parents had also learned from experience with his older siblings that kids will sometimes create alternative accounts without informing their parents. They will observe to see if he has little or no activity in his account, which is a tip he may have created a new account without telling them.)

Finally, with new social media apps appearing every month, Nathan's parents let him know he needed to ask permission whenever creating a new account or trying to download a new app. They would need to understand his intentions, the nature of the app, and/or why he needed yet another social media outlet. His father enabled the password-protected parental controls on Nathan's phone to limit his ability to download new apps or purchase anything through his smartphone. This forced a healthy conversation whenever there was a desire to try the latest and greatest app.

Knowing Nathan would soon be at an age when he could download apps at his own discretion, they wanted to teach him to think through certain questions before deciding to add an app to his device. They wanted him to wrestle with simple questions such as "What are the benefits of this app?" and

"What are the potential risks or downfalls of adding this app?" After having the app for a few weeks, they encouraged him to evaluate how important or necessary the app was to him. "Is this app adding value to my life or just taking up my time (and phone storage)?"

Nathan's mom was intentional in modeling how she ran through these same questions for herself when choosing apps. After a friend raved about a new app to help busy moms organize better, she asked herself the same questions before downloading it. After a few weeks, however, she noticed she rarely remembered to use the app as it was intended and it was taking up some of her phone's memory. She decided to delete the app. By modeling this process with your tween and teen son, you can equip them to become independent and discerning with their personal technology.

What are the consequences and rewards if social media is abused or used correctly?

Nathan's folks kept the consequences pretty clear and simple: Depending on the infraction, he would either need to shut down his account and/or lose his smartphone for a period of time.

- Minor issues would involve a day or two off his Instagram account.

- More serious issues would involve a week or more of losing his phone and staying out of his account.

- Serious safety concerns meant he would completely lose the privilege of having a social media account and using a smartphone until he was older and demonstrated more responsibility. Instead, they would replace his smartphone with a "dumb phone" (which had no internet, data, or text plan) to be used for cell calls only.

Since having a social media account was determined to be a privilege in itself, they agreed the reward for responsible behavior would be the ability to keep using Instagram and perhaps create other accounts on additional social networks in the future.

"What Movies Can I Watch? What Songs Can I Download? What Games Can I Play?"

Meet Sam, an eleven-year-old fifth-grader who is convinced his parents are "the worst" because they won't let him watch PG-13 movies. He insists all of his friends get to watch them, and some have even seen R-rated movies. Even worse, they won't let him download or stream the most popular hip-hop songs. And to top it all off, they will only let him play games rated "E" for everyone. Boring! He keeps asking, begging, and complaining, but so far he's had no luck convincing his parents to change their minds.

Sam's mom is not crazy about television, movies, games, or pop music. She admits she is rather conservative and would prefer Sam not be exposed to any of this media. The more she looks into the content and themes of the music and films, the less impressed she is. For these reasons, she is completely convinced that most of these requests are privileges to be earned later, when Sam is older and more mature. Sam's mom is getting really good at saying no for now.

What are the added responsibilities associated with this privilege?

Because Sam's parents are not allowing his requested privileges at this time, the nature of this question shifts to something more like "What responsibilities must Sam demonstrate in order to earn the privileges he wants?" As they discussed their decision, they clarified several things they expect.

First, they expect him to stop fussing and complaining, and to respect their decision. They have told him he can begin watching PG-13 movies when he turns thirteen. It is their belief that these ratings are there for a reason. In terms of music, they expect him to seek permission before he downloads new songs. His mother will use an online resource, such as commonsensemedia.org or pluggedin.com, to review the music Sam is requesting and let him know what he can and cannot buy. His mother has extended this rule to gaming as well, noticing that teen games are becoming increasingly sexualized and violent. She goes to sites like esrb.org (Entertainment Software Rating Board) to learn more about the games Sam wants to purchase and play.

In the end, they want Sam to demonstrate the maturity to have thoughtful conversations about the stories being told, the themes being presented, the choices being made in these forms of media. They want him to have a chance to define and establish his own moral compass before the entertainment industry inserts its powerful influence.

Consider one smart technique shared by a twelve-year-old boy. "My mom has this wonderful way of getting through. She doesn't say, 'You should' when I need help with a decision, but 'Have you considered . . . ?' or 'Maybe this would work . . .'

ARP *Adage*

Sometimes the best response is to answer a question with another question, like, "What do you think makes the most sense?" or "What are the options?" Questions like these will encourage your son to think on his own and to come to better conclusions.

giving me the final choice. And she lets me try things with just enough encouragement until I sort things out."

What are the consequences and rewards if this privilege is abused or used correctly by Sam?

- If Sam can respect their decision and honor these boundaries defined by his parents, he will earn their trust and the privilege to consume more sophisticated media as he matures.

- If he does not follow these guidelines, he will lose the privilege of watching any movies or playing video games with his friends. His parents agreed to start by enforcing these consequences for a week if he is caught breaking the rules. They will extend to multiple weeks if the irresponsible behavior continues.

We (the Larsons) attended a marriage and family conference and heard some powerful thoughts about parenting. Dr. Pat Love was giving a plenary address for the National Association of Relationship and Marriage Education (NARME). Her overarching point was that parents need to "make adulthood look attractive to young people." As she unpacked this premise, she talked about the relationship between responsibilities and privileges. Traditionally, one earns more privileges as one grows up and demonstrates increasing responsibility. You earn the privilege of driving a car by demonstrating the knowledge and skill needed to pass the driver's exam. Or, you get to drive when you have a part-time job and can help contribute to gas and insurance bills.

But our Western culture has begun to turn this around; the reaction is to say yes to everything. We give kids all sorts of privileges and none of the responsibility. Kids get to go where adults go, use the same powerful technology, drive nice cars, wear expensive fashionable clothes, and have access to an endless stream of entertainment. If we say yes to everything a child wants, what incentive is there to grow up? Why would I want to get a job and move out of the house someday if I get every privilege an adult has now and nothing is expected of me?

One option is to say no sometimes. "No, you can't join us for dinner tonight. We are going out for a date." "No, you can't get your driver's license until you find a part-time job and can help pay for gas." "No, I'm not buying you the latest smartphone." The premise is adults should have things and do things that kids can't until they begin to grow up and earn those privileges for themselves. Make adulthood look like something to aspire toward. Occasionally your son should be saying, "I can't wait until I grow up so I can . . ."

Remember to make adulthood look attractive. There may be certain decisions you make that he doesn't like. That's okay. You're sure to hear the old pleas for equity as he bargains against what his friends or older siblings get, but don't cave too quickly. If everything comes easily, we don't learn hard work and responsibility. Over time, he'll take great pride and satisfaction in earning privileges and demonstrating a mature level of responsibility. A new type of comparison will start to emerge as he notices the lack of responsibility (and gratitude) in his peers.

Some Final Comments About Technology: Embrace Your Limits

As we write this chapter, thousands of new apps are being developed. New apps coming out allow you to post questions, connect with strangers, post anonymous confessions, participate in sexual conversations, stream live video of yourself, post videos, and send messages that supposedly disappear after a certain amount of time. The danger and risks are obvious, and by the time you're reading this book, there will be even more dangerous functionality in the mobile app landscape.

As a parent, you can't screen every app. Nobody can keep up with all of the nuances of the ever-changing technology. Embrace your limits. Perhaps a better solution is to equip your son with some overarching principles that should guide his decisions. I (Heather) am reminded of my classroom when I was a fifth-grade teacher. Rather than come up with ninety-nine classroom rules to cover every situation I could think of (a lost cause anyhow), I would have a conversation with the students about two overarching rules for how we would carry ourselves in the class: safely and respectfully. I wanted the kids to think about their choices and consider if what they were doing was safe and respectful. Teaching them to apply these values to any situation that arose allowed us to deal with every interaction from cheating, bullying, running in the classroom, or talking out of turn. How might this principled approach apply to your son and technology?

If our sons learn to ask themselves what is *safe* when it comes to dealing with strangers in the digital world, we can educate them about the risks and help them make better decisions as new scenarios arise. And if they can remember what it means to *respect* themselves and others in what they say or post online, we can address a myriad of social media interactions with one simple rule.

Another technology challenge we face as parents is the effort to lock down all devices to prevent access to obscene or violent digital content, via parental controls, software filters, and passwords you can apply to phones and computers. We have nothing against these approaches; in fact, we use several of them ourselves. But at the end of the day, most teens can get around almost anything we put in place. The only foolproof choice is

ARP *Adage*

Remember, when dealing with any major issue, your influence as the parent is directly related to the relationship you have with your adolescent.

to get rid of all devices and then hope your child doesn't glance too closely at their friend's smartphone.

Again, we encourage you to embrace your limits and have a conversation with your tween about character and the choices they will make when nobody is looking. Believing your son is becoming a godly young man will help you encourage him to make wise choices and show grace when he makes mistakes. Remember he is learning. He is a work in progress. He has not arrived. When he makes mistakes, you can show grace and understanding. You have not failed as a parent. Yelling and shaming him will not help him learn and grow. Understanding and love will help him trust you when he is struggling again to make wise choices with technology. Focus instead on helping him put into place accountability as he continues to grow into a godly young man. It may start with a break from all technology for a bit. Then as the privilege of technology is reintroduced, ask him, "What will help you avoid temptation in the future?" In the spirit of this book, we suggest that regular conversations about temptations, accountability, and good decisions may be a more effective and empowering approach than trying to chase down every privacy setting you can find.

1. "When do I get a smartphone?" You may hesitate to bring up this question if it's not already being asked in your home. Be sure, the question is coming! Talking with your tween may end unnecessary begging in the future.

2. "How will social media be used in our home?" Find out what social media your son is thinking about. Talk about the responsibilities associated with social media and your expectations.

3. "What movies can I watch? What songs can I download? Which games can I play?" These questions provide opportunities to hear what music, movies, and games your son is interested in. Take time to explore his media and talk about what you see and hear together.

(Additional questions for each topic)

What are the added responsibilities associated with this privilege?

What are the consequences and rewards if this privilege is abused or used correctly?

Conversation 5

• • •

THE FAITH TALK

Internalizing Values

When we asked parents "What do you want the most for your son?" some of the answers we received were:

- "That we would always have a healthy, open relationship with good communication."
- "That my son would own his own personal faith in God."
- "That my son would find a spouse with similar values—that family would always be important to him."
- "That my tween would know what he believes and would base his life on sound biblical principles."
- "That my son would be a well-adjusted adult and contribute to the betterment of this world."
- "That my teenager would be able to stand strong and make wise choices."

When considering the big issues of life, we didn't hear parents make comments like "I hope my son will always have a clean room and brush his teeth" or "I hope my son will never pierce his lip and get tattoos."

What do you think of when you look at the big picture? If you were to write a sentence or two on what you desire for your son, what would you write?

Ben grew up in a home as the youngest of three siblings. His older brothers were eight and ten years his senior. This gap in age provided an interesting perspective from which to observe their spiritual journeys. For while he was still in a very concrete stage of faith development, he saw his older brothers question, resist, leave, and then return to their family's faith tradition. His brothers' beliefs were no longer identical to his parents', but they had arrived at a solid spot. It was all quite bewildering to the younger Ben, and yet it somehow normalized the process of moving through his own journey of faith development.

The challenge in the area of faith and spirituality is for kids to transition from *borrowing* their parents' faith to *owning* their own journey. It is super important to educate and expose children to the family's faith tradition, but at some point your son will make a decision for himself about what he believes.

ARP *Adage*

Consider this: If you trust God with your life, then trust God to help you with your son who is on his own personal faith journey. We were able to keep going when we hit rough places because we knew God was totally committed to us and to our children in transition. We reminded each other what the psalmist wrote: "The Lord will perfect that which concerns me" (Psalm 138:8 NKJV).

Keep in mind his journey is just beginning, and he is still a work in progress. With so many transitions happening in terms of brain development, cognitive abilities, social life, and hormones, don't expect him to have his whole theological worldview figured out at this age.

"Who Do You Believe God Is?"

This is a big question, and how it is answered affects the very foundations and direction of our lives. Faith informs our identity, values, and decisions on multiple facets of life, including finances, education, relationships, leisure, and vocation.

James W. Fowler, a developmental psychologist, wrote extensively about the stages of faith development in his book *Stages of Faith*. The model can be helpful in understanding some of what your child may be experiencing. While he outlines a seven-stage process from birth to older age, we'll look at the stages most relevant to tweens.[1]

Stage 1: According to Fowler's model, preschool-aged children (three to seven years old) are in Stage 1 of faith development and tend to learn about God through their experiences, images, stories, and people in their life. Sunday school classes for young children are designed around crafts, stories, and experiential Bible learning. In this stage, children reflect what they are taught and exposed to, mostly by their parents.

Stage 2: The next stage develops in school-age children from about seven to twelve years old. Kids in this stage will often have strong beliefs around justice and the reciprocity of the universe. They become more concrete about what they consider right and wrong, good and bad, and so on. This stage of faith development coincides with another famous developmental model created by Swiss psychologist Jean Piaget. One of his stages of cognitive development in children ages seven to eleven is called the *concrete operational stage*, which is marked by more logical thinking. The limitation, however, is that kids in this stage of cognitive development tend to be quite rigid in their thinking and struggle with more abstract concepts. Metaphors and symbolic language associated with religion are sometimes misunderstood. Somewhat like Santa Claus, God is likely perceived as a white-haired old man who is distant, keeping track of good and bad behavior, and not very involved in his life.

Stage 3: Your tween son may be starting to move into Stage 3 of his developmental faith journey, which typically begins around age twelve and will often last throughout adolescence. Thinking in this stage advances as kids begin to understand more abstract concepts. Boys in this stage have a deepening concern for others' point of view and a growing interest in interpersonal relationships. The increasing importance of significant relationships is reflected in their faith as they now have the capacity for a more personal relationship with God, whom they may perceive as a cooperating friend.[2]

In summary, your son is on a faith journey that may evolve from a simplistic reflection of what he's seen and heard in your family, to a Santa-like old man who keeps score of right and wrong, and finally to a loving friend who is interested in his daily life. The model is a general overview, and not every boy will have the same experience or timing described above. Still, it is helpful to have some sense of the typical development faith journey so you can recognize some of the behavior and thinking you're seeing unfold in his life.

This question, "Who do you believe God is?" is indeed a big one. Remember, he is developmentally in somewhat of a bind.

Part of him will feel the social pressures to conform, while his newly developing cognitive abilities can begin to question the status quo. If your son struggles to answer this big question, consider following up with additional prompts such as:

- What do you picture when you think of God?
- How does God respond to your prayers?
- What role does God play in your daily life?
- How does God make a difference in your world?

It is important to make room for doubts. Some church traditions imply that doubts or questions are a sign of a weak faith and should be squelched. Research, however, shows that as many as 70 percent of teens have questions about God and faith. Unfortunately, less than half of these students raise their questions with a friend, parent, or youth leader. When we accept and welcome questions as a normal part of faith development and provide young people with a safe environment to ask their questions or express their doubts, they actually feel more supported by their parents and by God.[3]

Doubt is not the absence of faith, but rather the obstacle to overcome in order to experience faith. Knowledge is the opposite of faith. Think about this: When I (Heather) know a certain tree is an oak tree, then I also know what kind of leaves and bark it has. It requires no faith for me to believe the tree is an oak. Doubt is actually part of faith. For instance, I believe my husband loves me. I feel his love, and he does many things that show me love. Sometimes when he is frustrated or disappointed, I can doubt his love, but I choose to believe that even in his frustration, he still loves me. Believing is choosing to overcome the doubt. We don't have to be afraid when our tweens experience doubt. Instead, listen and ask them questions about God's faithfulness and love in the past. As they get to know God better, they will be able to know Him even in the confusing times, when it's hard to feel God's love or faithfulness.

"How Will You Continue to Pursue Your Faith?"

What are your hopes and desires for your son's personal faith? How will he own his spiritual disciplines such as prayer, tithing, and serving? What truths would you like to communicate to him? One friend, Gail, wrote each of her children a letter with her goals and desires for their spiritual growth. The kids read and re-read these letters of encouragement over and over through their teen years.

I (Heather) was super involved in church and youth group as a teen. I was *doing* everything right: attending youth group, volunteering, singing in the choir, and attending church every Sunday. You could find me at church more days of the week than not. I knew all of the right answers and believed them too. I just didn't know *why*.

My first year at college, when I took out my Bible, my roommate asked, "Why do you believe that, anyway?" Before this time, I had not stopped to ask myself that question. My only response was an uncertain reply: "Because my parents told me to?" Needless to say, I was still *borrowing* my family's faith.

ARP *Adage*

A wise friend reminded us, "If my kids buy in to 90 percent of my value system, I will feel I have done a good job of passing on my faith." Our children are not clones. They will go places we will not go and experience things we will not experience. Life goes forward, not backward.

During the college years, I was actively (and at other times, not so actively) exploring what my faith meant to me. I needed to know for myself why I wanted to read the Bible and who God was in my life. I know this time of questioning and uncertainty was difficult for my parents to watch. Their patience and prayer without pressure allowed me to discover and eventually *own* the faith I have today.

Maybe you've heard the expression, "God doesn't have any grandchildren, just children." The shift from a parent's faith to son's faith is an important rite of passage. In a way, he *borrows* his parents' religion until he is old enough to think critically and form his own opinions and belief structures. In time, he'll ask more questions, push back on the old answers, try on different ideas, and consider the grays in what used to be a very black and white world. Some boys do this very overtly and assertively, while others will quietly process all of this on an internal level. The questions for this conversation should help you begin to get a read on where your son is at on his journey.

One task for a parent will be to make this unfolding process okay and embrace the normal questioning taking place, without receiving it as a rejection or slap in the face. You may have already heard some of the questions: "Why does God let bad things happen to good people?" "If God already knows what is going to happen, what difference do my personal choices make?" "What difference will my prayers make to God?" "Where does it say that in the Bible?" and "Who wrote the Bible? Is it really the Word of God? How do we know it is accurate?"

Sometimes our urge in the face of our son's ambivalent questioning is to rush in and reassure him, attempting to provide solid answers and shore up the foundations we've tried to instill in the formation of his belief structures. Unfortunately, the more a parent advances their experience of the truth, the more it can actually backfire as it simply gives him more to push against.

Take heart, however—it is a normal and often necessary phase of his development. Instead, encourage your son to explore the answers to tough questions. Sticky Faith Curriculum published *Can I Ask That?* as a resource with a small group discussion for teens to explore just such topics.[4]

Letting Go and Letting God

As children transition into adolescence, parents need to transition from directing to facilitating spiritual growth. Scary as it seems, you need to help move your preteen from living by your family rules and standards to living by their own personal inner convictions. As a mom who is also a youth leader says:

> Having expectations of kids is extremely important. Our kids know we expect certain things of them. For example, they know we want to see them walking with the Lord, obeying, helping and respecting our family, looking out for the needs of others, and being honest. While we are not ignorant to the fact our kids might make foolish choices, we understand talking negatively about teens somehow gives them permission to be foolish. By calling them up to a higher standard, we are hoping they rise to the occasion.

To facilitate personal spiritual growth, you need to help your son move from dependence on you the parent to dependence on God. This transition is not a science—there are not ten easy steps to helping kids grow spiritually and no guarantees that they will choose your personal convictions. You cannot legislate spiritual growth and maturity, but you can do what you can and put the rest in God's hands.

It's hard to relax when you feel responsible for things you can't control. It's hard to watch your tween struggle with faith issues. During these years it's good to remember the serenity prayer: "Grant me the serenity to accept the things I cannot change, the courage to change the things I can, and the wisdom to know the difference."

One dad used to stare at that prayer, which was displayed on the wall of his church. On some level he knew it was true, but he didn't want to admit that there were things in his life he could not control. Finally, he realized that so many things in his life were so out of control that he had to take the leap of faith and relax and trust God for what he couldn't control.

While parents may not be able to *control* their son's faith journey, they can certainly *influence* it. We (the Larsons) have found resources outside of our home that can speak into our son's life. Youth groups and small groups at church allow adult volunteers and peers to unpack some of these difficult questions in a safe and loving environment. Parachurch organizations such as Young Life or Fellowship of Christian Athletes allow kids to explore faith in the context of their peers from school and engaging young adult volunteers. Even a week or two of summer camp, offered through a trusted organization, can provide powerful and transformative experiences for your son outside of his normal home environment. Maybe there is a book or an app that would help him on his journey. Pay attention and give him opportunities to explore his faith at a safe distance.

Don't underestimate the influence of family devotions. One friend shared how she had provided devotional material to her son that was age appropriate and attractive to tweens. For her son, who enjoyed baseball and fishing, they liked *Playing With a Purpose: Baseball Devotions* by Paul Kent, and *Catch of the Day* by Jimmy Houston. *Take a Turn for God in Just 5 Minutes a Day*, by Blaine Bartel, is a more generic devotional that would appeal to most teen boys. Ask your son's youth leader, or even look online. The important thing is to provide options that will engage your son.

"What Are Our Family's Expectations for Church Attendance and Activities?"

Our friends the Johnsons shared a typical Sunday morning in their house with their two sons, Alex, age twelve, and Paul, age fourteen. On a typical Sunday morning at seven, the house is still quiet. Their sons are fast asleep because they were up late playing games, watching movies, and hanging out with friends. The Johnsons face a decision: church or no church today? They know if they wake the boys up and begin to rally the troops for church, it is probably going to turn into a battle. There will be complaining, stalling, and overall resistance. They've heard it before: "Church is boring!" "I don't like that youth group—none of my friends are there." "Seriously, that music is the worst!"

It used to be easier. The Johnsons remember when their sons gladly went to church. The boys woke up early, even before their parents, and were ready for the day. They were happy to go to Sunday school and hear the Bible stories and play games. Sometimes there were even doughnuts or bagels in the church lobby to provide the perfect reward for being at church. Now, however, they want to sleep in late. They are full of reasons to skip, and may even have other activities or sports that compete with Sunday mornings.

The parents have to cajole the boys into taking a shower and wearing nicer clothes. They may or may not have time to eat breakfast, and the whole family is stressed because they are all typically running late by the time they finally get out the door. Still, the Johnsons want to do their best because they desire to raise their boys up in the traditions and teachings dear to their hearts. It is often tempting to avoid the battle altogether and let everyone sleep in. But they remember the promises they made at their sons' dedications, before the entire congregation, to raise them up *in the nurture and admonition of the Lord.*

For many, the scenario described above is familiar. But for some families, the flip side of the coin is true. Perhaps you are not connected to a church or place of worship, but now you have a child who wants to go. Maybe you had a negative church experience growing up and you've grown to generally mistrust religious institutions. But his school friends have invited him to attend an active church in your community, and he likes it! This might feel unsettling and raise your concerns about the ideas and teachings to which he'll be introduced. How might this disrupt the normal flow of your family?

At what age does he get to begin to make these decisions for himself? It may begin to sound redundant, but your tween son will increasingly want to control his own faith journey (and practices) as he grows up. For families who are trying to instill a faith tradition to a resistant tween, it can be helpful to give him some options that empower him with certain choices he can make for himself:

- Maybe he wants to sit with his friends in the balcony during the worship service.

- Perhaps he wants to attend the contemporary service rather than the traditional.

- Some tweens enjoy stepping up to volunteer with various aspects of the church (e.g., helping on the setup team or being part of the worship band) and they are old enough to do it on their own.

Sometimes the choices will even stretch you further. We've seen kids who want to attend a different church from their parents because the traditional service does not feel as relevant to them as the upbeat service and vibrant youth group offered elsewhere. Some tweens are willing to attend a Sunday morning service with their parents but would rather plug in with a parachurch youth organization instead of their church's standard youth group. Perhaps your son will choose to explore some facet of his faith that is outside your comfort zone. It can be difficult to predict his path, so be ready to be stretched!

You'll need to decide what is required, recommended, or totally optional when it comes to church attendance. For those things you want to require as a parent, consider ways to communicate this message without being harsh or punitive. Once you've clarified the expectations, ask him how he feels about your standards in this area. Is he in agreement? Does he feel your expectations are reasonable? If he is struggling with what's been decided, try to empathize and keep the dialogue going.

Friday Pancakes

One of the best situations we (the Arps) experienced was when we were living in Vienna, Austria. Several wrestlers with an organization called Athletes in Action took an interest in our sons and in helping them reach out to their friends. Here's how it started. We were in a small congregation with no youth group so we offered to begin one in our home. Every other Friday after school our teens invited their friends from school to come to our house for what became known as "Friday Pancakes." (Once the group was established we substituted popcorn for pancakes. It wasn't so messy and much simpler!)

The wrestlers took turns leading Friday Pancakes. Skits, table tennis, videos, and short talks on how your values system and faith can affect your life as a teenager were among the activities. But basically, the group was about having fun and providing a positive environment for our teenagers. The group grew, and we achieved one of our goals of providing a positive peer group for our teens as well as great role models. Years later we are still in touch with those inspiring wrestlers through Facebook.

Let us add, just in case you think relating to adolescents was easy for us, that when we first entered this stage of family life, we were very ill at ease with this age group. But this was a priority in our family so we worked hard to relate to our adolescents and to their friends. We did what we could to get our children into a positive peer group. We invested in them and their friends and had an open-home policy. We even spent extra time and money to give rides to sports, scouts, and youth groups. Trust us, it is not always easy, but you can do it. Do your best to be available and flexible.

From Standards to Convictions

Christian parents naturally desire to see their children grow in their relationship with God. This is something you can influence but not control. As children grow older, wise parents lead by example—by praying for their children and allowing them the freedom to internalize their faith so that they can make choices based on their own inner convictions rather than just on your family's rules and standards.

Ultimately they must choose their own convictions, but how can you help influence their choices? Think about this: A person is not free to choose God's way as his own until he is given the choice. A belief must be chosen freely. What if your son makes a wrong choice? While it's hard to watch this process, it is healthier than to watch him as an older adolescent struggle because he was never given the gift of personal choices. So he enters a new world, no longer surrounded by parental influence and without strong convictions of his own. That can spell confusion and heartache in terms of experimentation and trying to sift through all kinds of new philosophies. How much better to form basic convictions while still at home.

We encourage you to begin to take baby steps at shifting the responsibility for your son's spiritual life from your shoulders to his. Here are some suggestions for beginning that shift:

- *Encourage your son to ask questions.* Sometimes he may ask questions that will really surprise you. Most families have at least one resident cynic, and we (the Arps) were no exception. While we did not always have the answers, we tried to help find them. Remember, your adolescent must find answers. Years ago when we were growing up, a strong moral code undergirded the educational system. Now kids face hot issues in school like abortion, same-sex marriage, premarital sex, drugs, alcohol, gender-related questions, and so on. If you don't help answer their questions, someone else surely will.

- *Provide good resources for your child.* If your tween requests your help in purchasing good literature, apps, or other faith-building resources, be willing to help purchase them.

- *Look for mentors for your tween.* Young adults can influence your child in positive ways. Church youth groups, Christian camps, and conferences are great places to find a mentor for your son. This is especially helpful during those years when parents seem to lose all their intelligence and credibility with their own children.

- *Be a good role model.* We can't say we were always great role models, but we tried to be. We weren't always consistent, but over the years we consistently tried to be consistent. Sometimes our ideas worked, and other times we hoped that our common sense would get us through the difficult times.

- *Trust God for what you don't yet see!* We were able to keep going during the hard times because we knew God was totally committed to us and to our family. How do we know this? Re-read Psalm 138:8 (NKJV): "The Lord will perfect that which concerns me." When you need hope for the future, remember verses like Romans 8:25—"But if we hope for what we do not yet have, we wait for it patiently"—and 1 Corinthians 9:10 (NKJV)—"He who plows should plow in hope." If you have a good concordance you can find a list of all the Bible verses that contain the word *hope*. When you feel discouraged, read through some of these verses.

- *Pray for your child.* Parenthood is not a solitary occupation. We have a backup in the resources of the living God. Talk to Him often about your children!

1. "Who do you believe God is?" Let your son explore this question with you. You will learn about his heart and be able to share yours too.

2. "How will you continue to pursue your faith?" Giving your son the opportunity to own his faith is a big step, but is necessary to make his faith his own. You can ask how you might help him continue to grow in his faith. Would he like a devotional book or other resource? Does he have a Bible that is age appropriate?

3. "What are our family's expectations for church attendance and activities?" Even though it may feel early to talk about this topic, you'll be glad you've brought it up so when the time comes it won't be such a battle.

Online Resources:

www.stickyfaith.org

Conversation 6

...

THE ACADEMICS TALK

Academic Pressure/Stress

Mom confronting her son who got a less-than-stellar grade in Spanish class:

"What is this C all about?"

Son to mom: "Well, the classroom is too small and the teacher is not very good."

Mom: "Really?"

Son: "Yeah, plus the work is way harder this year than it was last year!"

You may chuckle because you've heard the excuses before. Maybe you even tried some of them when you were a student. But if your son gets all As and Bs in school except for a C in Spanish, what do you spend the most time talking about? Sure, he needs to work on Spanish, but perhaps your son is just not great with foreign languages. After all, as one twelve-year-old son told his mom, "You can know over half of the material and still get an F."

Some may not like the direction we're taking for this conversation about school and academics. Our focus is more about developing as a whole person rather than developing a high GPA. It is a long-term perspective that assumes well-rounded kids will grow up to be successful adults. More and more we've come to believe that a degree from a particular school is not what matters most. I (Peter) have worked as both a departmental director and president of a successful company. In these roles, I've had to hire people and occasionally terminate an individual's employment. I can tell you from experience that character, work ethic, emotional intelligence, and leadership ability are just some of the factors we valued as much as or more than a degree from the "right" college.

It is not that we don't care about succeeding in school, but the overemphasis on grades can be too narrow and place undue pressure on kids. As you'll see as this chapter unfolds, we argue

ARP *Adage*

Initially, girls tend to adjust better to school and read sooner than boys do. In the early elementary years, boys can be more aggressive and excel at gross motor skills (like throwing and catching). Girls are typically better at fine motor skills (drawing or handwriting) and excel verbally. While girls can begin puberty as early as nine or ten, boys usually begin puberty around eleven or twelve or even later.

During early puberty, boys tend to have a harder time academically than girls. Try to be patient and help them avoid thinking of themselves as less intelligent. Boys' brain development is simply different from girls', and as late developers, they might not yet have the same mental capacity of their same-age female peers and will need a little more time. In the long run, things will settle down and they will catch up.

that school can be a rich environment for learning much more than just academic facts.

I (Peter) remember showing my report card to my father when I was a sophomore in high school. I had just completed a particularly successful semester and was bringing home mostly As. I'll never forget my father's response as he looked at my grades and, after pausing, said, "Why don't you relax a little bit . . . get some Bs." Wow! This was not the response I had expected, but in retrospect it makes a lot of sense.

While eventually earning a master's degree in social work, my dad had been a C student throughout high school. He was more athletic than academic and spent more time with friends than books. His strategic thinking and relational aptitude, however, had served him well as an adult, and he eventually founded and ran a very successful business.

From his vantage point, my good grade in Algebra II was not as important as a manageable stress level. His life experience had taught him that high grades were not the lone predictor of success. I was fortunate because this type of parental climate took the pressure off. I was internally motivated to achieve, and my father knew this, so there was no need for him to add unneeded expectations or pressure to my life.

Mary asked her seventh-grade son, Aaron, what he liked most about school. His quick response was, "My friends." Mary then asked him what he thought the goal of school was. Aaron's response was, "To learn stuff." When asked about why you learn stuff, Aaron said, "So you can be prepared for life." Mary thought this was a pretty solid answer, so she proceeded to ask if there was anything that gets in the way of "learning stuff," and she could only laugh as Aaron's immediate answer was again, "My friends."

Interesting. His favorite thing about school is also the very thing he perceives gets in the way of learning. Obviously there are some things Mary could address about disruptions or distractions coming from friends. But there may also be room for Aaron to expand his ideas about the purpose of school and realize that his relationships with friends can play an important role in his future.

"What Is the Goal of School?"

How often do we stop and consider this question? What is the end goal when it comes to school and education? When we really pause and reflect on these questions, we may be surprised that we've bought into a cultural lie. Consider the logical conclusions of the following hypothetical conversation between a parent and teen:

> "You need to work harder on that assignment."
>
> "Why?"
>
> "So you'll get a good grade."
>
> "Why?"
>
> "So you'll have a good GPA."
>
> "Why?"
>
> "So you'll be able to get into a good college."
>
> "Why?"
>
> "So you'll be able to land a good job."
>
> "Why?"
>
> "So you can make lots of money."
>
> "Why?"
>
> "So you can buy a house, own a car, and lead a comfortable life."
>
> Teen responds, "What if that's not what I want?"

Is comfort the main goal of education (or even of life)? Surely there is more to schooling than making enough money to be comfortable. We now live in a world where it is becoming fashionable to own a tiny house, ride your bike, and plan to work well into old age rather than aspire for retirement. The old assumptions do not hold up for the younger generations. The old appeals for success and comfort may not even be attractive to young people today.

Still, many families just plod along in the educational system without ever asking *why* or *what is the end goal*. As we look deeper into the common goals of the Western educational system, however, we are pleased to see some of the articulated objectives go well beyond academic achievement and can equip your son to lead a very fulfilling life.

Social and Emotional Development

An important artifact of school is the social interactions that kids experience. Learning how to handle conflict, deal with a demanding teacher, or navigate the politics of a clique are actually important life skills. Later in life, these skills will help your son solve problems with co-workers, deal with a tough boss, manage stress, and navigate his adult social life with increased confidence. Kids in school figure out how to interact with a range of personalities, ignore distractions, and foster close friendships. They are put in situations where they must work in teams or deliver a project working alone.

Consider the playground dynamics your son experiences in elementary school. Kids on the playground need to navigate who they will play with and who they will keep at a distance. The very act of choosing teams for a game of kickball presents all sorts of challenges. They learn to manage their anger, survive hurtful situations, lead discussions, negotiate rules, settle disputes, and laugh with friends. There are usually ups and downs in this social and emotional development process, but school is one of the few places where parents are typically removed from the situation, forcing kids to find their own way.

Tyler is a twelve-year-old who is being homeschooled, a path that used to be equated with poor socialization. These days, however, his mom takes him to a homeschool group two days per week, providing opportunities for his social and emotional development with peers. This is an important development in the culture of homeschooling.

In a recent survey, CareerBuilder.com asked more than 2,600 hiring managers about their practices and found that 71 percent valued emotional intelligence over IQ. They believe those with higher emotional intelligence can handle high pressure, resolve conflict, lead by example, show empathy, and make more thoughtful decisions. In fact, 75 percent of managers said they are more likely to promote someone with higher emotional intelligence.[1]

Citizenship

It is easy to overlook the opportunities a student has for learning about leadership and service at school. Through activities like student council, clubs, sports teams, fundraisers, and service projects, students are exposed to several important learning opportunities that are independent of academic achievement. They begin to identify and articulate the things they care about. Participating in these activities can give them firsthand experience with skills such as public communication, strategic planning, teamwork, organization, and leadership. These activities help them practice their people skills in real-world situations that translate well to community and occupational situations they will face as adults.

Vocational Preparation: Competing in a Global Workforce

When we (the Larsons) moved to a new school district in Minnesota and enrolled our children in school, we were surprised to learn they would need to have laptop computers because all of their classes and homework were to be completed on the computer. We were not against this, but it was out of our usual paradigm. As parents, we want to be careful about fostering too much screen time. But in a world where both business and higher education are so reliant on computers, perhaps we should be grateful our schools are pushing computers and tablets into the daily academic flow. Nationwide, more schools are beginning to leverage technology and adapt course work to better prepare students for relevant career paths. Some foster work-based learning programs that actually allow students to earn academic credits while working part-time through arranged apprenticeships or school-based enterprises. It is not an uncommon assignment for high school students to contact, interview, and shadow adults in the workforce to learn more about potential careers. These types of innovations speak to the role of school in preparing kids to enter the competitive global workforce.

Cognitive Growth

Perhaps the most obvious role of school is to foster learning. School education exposes kids to mountains of information, challenging them to understand, remember, and apply it. School should challenge your son to develop his study habits, memory, critical thinking, creativity, logic, and focus.

With these common goals in mind, it may be helpful to have your son think about what his own personal goals for school could be. Does he have a sense of what he wants to do for a career? Does he know what he wants to major in at college? Is he solid academically but needs to work on making friends? Is he intelligent but has a hard time applying good study habits? Help him begin to think through how he can get the most out of school. If he doesn't yet have a plan, don't stress out about it. While some kids seem to just know what they want to do at an early age, most take several more years to begin defining a direction.

Still, his choices in the next few years may impact his ability to accomplish certain goals. Boys in the tween and teen years are most focused on the moment and often are not thinking through how their choices today will impact the future. If his goal is to attend a college with the help of a scholarship, he may want to see what qualifications are required to receive such a scholarship. Colleges often are looking to see a well-rounded student instead of just academic achievement. Thinking through what other activities to participate in now will help him round out who he is growing into during these years.

"What Gets in the Way of These Goals?"

There are several variables that can interfere with your son's ability to achieve his goals for school.

Finding the Balance Between Too Narrow or Too Broad

If the only goals are good grades, then everything else could be considered an obstacle that competes with academic success. A single goal that focuses only on grades may be too narrow, neglecting other areas of a balanced life. As humans, we tend to focus on the areas where we feel successful and avoid things that are uncomfortable. While some boys will major in friends or sports and avoid their studies, others can hide in their books and avoid social interactions as much as possible.

Often it is the parent, and not the child, who is overly focused on grades. Research suggests pressure is greater when parents focus mainly on the external rather than internal reasons for success.[2] In other words, if children hear the message they must do well in order to get into the best college and have a prominent career, the stakes are pretty high. On the other hand, if students connect to the enjoyment, curiosity, and personal satisfaction that comes with learning and achieving their potential, the messages are more balanced and the pressure more manageable.

Some families go too broad and have their sons involved in everything: sports, music, theatre, youth group, AP classes, and so on. While there are those amazing kids who seem to be able to do it all, focusing too broadly can create incredible stress. A certain driver of stress is to have more to do than you have time in which to accomplish it all. Sometimes it's kids who don't want to feel left out and sign up for everything they can. Other times it is well-intentioned parents who don't want their sons to miss out on any possible experience. Either way, going too broad can get in the way of doing fewer things with true excellence.

Finding a balance in life is key. Families need a balance between academics and other activities, but they also need to find balance in whose interests and energy drives the priorities. Josh had a gift for lacrosse. He was only eleven, but he distinguished himself on the field as unusually fast and fearless. His father was very excited about Josh's future in lacrosse and pushed him to try out for the twelve-year-olds' traveling team, even though he was a full year younger than the other boys. When he didn't make the team, the father was the one who was devastated. He pushed his son to practice more, hired a personal trainer, and contracted a private coach. Fast-forward three years and Josh quit lacrosse altogether, burned out by the pressure and unbalanced focus in his life. The priority expressed in his home had been sports, not school. He was behind in his studies and had to reapply himself at school in order to catch up.

Achievement vs Intelligence

An educational psychologist would tell you there is a distinct contrast between intelligence and achievement. Intelligence is the raw smarts a person possesses. When we talk about IQ, we are referring to one's *intelligence quotient* as indicated by a standardized test of some sort. Achievement, on the other hand, is what one accomplishes in terms of grades and daily successes. The moderating variables between these two concepts are tools like work ethic, organization, time-management, focus, and motivation.

Some students may not be as naturally gifted with smarts, but they overachieve simply because of their raw determination and drive. Others are extremely intelligent, but underachieve because they lack the work ethic, motivation, or time-management skills needed to get things done with excellence. Lack of these skills can certainly inhibit your son's ability to achieve his goals, no matter how smart he is. While you can't really change someone's basic IQ, you can teach skills that foster high achievement. One can learn to be more organized and better manage one's schedule. We can find ways to motivate an underachiever through various rewards and incentives.

ARP *Adage*

To build some of these foundational tools in our kids, we organized and hosted a study workshop led by an older student who had distinguished himself as a good student with a positive life balance. We are convinced our boys responded better to an upperclassman's tips than they would have to their parents' prodding and direction.

"What Helps You to Be Most Successful at School?"

Every student has a different academic personality when it comes to studying. This personality helps inform how your son will study and what parameters to put into place to help him be more successful. Ultimately, your end goal as a parent is to equip him to study and learn on his own, taking responsibility for his own success in education. When your son asks for help on an algebra problem, it is an opportunity to teach him to use resources to help him solve the problem (using the book or online math sites), not just help him get the right answer on that problem. I (Heather) often joke with the kids, "I won't be going off to college in your back pocket to help you, nor will you want me to!" It is important our boys are equipped to study, learn, and take responsibility for their education during the teen years.

When it comes to the best environment for school success, the answers will depend on your son's personality, goals, ability, and his work ethic.

You can think of your son's academic personality on a spectrum of sorts. And where he falls on this spectrum may dictate the best environment for him. Some boys are organized, goal-oriented, and super responsible when it comes to school. They are what you picture when you think of a straight-A student. If this is your son, perhaps his need is to avoid obsessing or putting too much pressure on himself. His home environment may need to encourage a balance between academics and well-rounded interests and meaningful friendships.

On the other end of the continuum are boys who are disorganized, distracted, and not very responsible. They lose things, forget their homework, and struggle to focus on school. Sports, friends, or video games overshadow any sense of urgency to achieve in school. The optimal home environment for this type of boy will need to introduce more structure and motivation. He may need to be pushed and challenged to remove distractions.

	ORGANIZED SON	DISORGANIZED SON
BEHAVIOR STYLE	Goal-oriented, super responsible, overachiever, may be stressed or anxious	Scattered, distracted, loses things, forgetful, unfocused
NEEDS FROM HOME	Encourage more balance, less pressure, set aside time for friendships	More structure, increased motivation through consequences and rewards, help removing distractions

One family shared how their two kids represented the various facets of this continuum. William (age twelve) almost couldn't relax until his homework was finished. When he arrived home from school, he sat down and did his homework immediately with an internal drive and focus that needed no prodding from adults. Paul (age fourteen) had always received good grades, but he could take thirty minutes of homework and make it last for hours, with several breaks and interactions that became time-consuming distractions. His parents often felt pulled to prod him into action or try to organize his efforts. In the end, however, they concluded they were not doing Paul any favors when they "over-functioned" for him.

A close family friend of ours has spoken words of wisdom on this topic of helping a less-organized child. He is a middle school science teacher who has been teaching for over a decade. In his experience, he has seen all sorts of students and all sorts of parents, but he is convinced that too many parents over-function for their middle school kids, working harder than the children themselves. While this approach may be well intentioned, it is only a short-term solution with long-term consequences.

One stressed son rushed into the kitchen and said, "Mom, I need help on my project!"

"What kind of project is it, honey?" his mother asked.

"It is a big social studies project. I'm supposed to create a map or model of an early colony, and I don't have any of the right supplies," he exclaimed.

"When is it due?" his mother asked.

"Tomorrow!" cried the son.

Learning through natural consequences can be very powerful. Doing poorly on a project, or even failing a test, can be powerful natural consequences that can wake some kids up and provide the motivation they need to begin making changes. But when parents rescue their middle school child by doing half their homework, completing their projects, and organizing their backpack each night, they are actually creating dependency. They are working harder than their child! Comparatively speaking, the stakes are pretty low in middle school as things like class rank and GPA are not tracked until high school. If a child is to learn important experiential lessons through failing, it is better it happens in sixth or seventh grade as compared with sophomore or junior year of high school. As mentioned throughout this book, our job is to hand over responsibility and let our sons own their journey. This is true in academics just as it is in faith or finances.

"How Do You Feel About Our Family's Expectations About Grades?"

What Do Grades Mean?

When placing a value on grades, it is important to understand what grades actually mean. As a former teacher, I (Heather) believe grades are a three-way means of communication. The grade communicates to the teacher what a student knows, and the teacher shares that information with the parent and student.

Some areas of content are mastered or understood while other areas of content may need to be reviewed again. Grades also communicate the level of effort and responsibility of the student. Several missing assignments but great test scores communicate that the knowledge and understanding is there, but the effort is lacking. Grades are not meant to be an identity, as in, "He is an A student" or "He is only a C student." They are simply a form of communication about one small slice of a child's life and performance.

Looking at grades as a means of communication helps students, teachers, and parents know where to focus. A student who is lacking in effort and responsibility does not need tutoring in the subject, but he may benefit from some external accountability to help him finish his work. On the other hand, the boy who has all of his work turned in but is struggling to master the content may benefit from tutoring or online help.

If you view grades as a means of communication, it opens up dialogue with your son. When he brings home a test, start by asking him questions. Let's say, for example, he received a 75 percent or a C on the test. I always start with, "How did you feel about the test?" This question provides a ton of insight. If he responds he thought the test was super easy, the C might indicate a need for further questions about what type of grades he is aiming for. Perhaps he will share he is embarrassed by the C grade. He had thought the test was going to be covering different information and was surprised when he found he had studied the wrong material.

Another question to ask him after a test is, "What would you do differently to prepare for the test next time?" Again, depending on the answer, you may want to follow up with, "How do you plan to implement that change?" Helping him get specific on how to prepare for future tests—not just letting the answer go at "study more, duh!"—will help him put together a specific plan (make notecards, try a pretest online, begin studying or working on the project sooner, study with fewer distractions, organize a study group, etc.).

Remember to focus on the positive grades too. Asking, "What are you most proud of on this test?" or asking, "What are you celebrating that you did well?" is a great way to encourage your son and let him see you recognize his efforts too. If he sees you acknowledge his positive efforts, it will increase his desire to keep it up!

Asking about academic expectations can be a loaded conversation. Where do your expectations come from? Are they realistic? Do they align with your son's gifts, interests, and goals? Has he bought in? Does he share your expectations?

Consider James, age twelve, who is attending a rigorous charter school, taking advanced classes, and working hard for his B average. He is smart but not necessarily gifted. His work ethic and time management allow him to achieve this solid GPA despite the challenging curriculum. His goal is to be the first in his family to graduate from a four-year college. Compare him with Blake, age thirteen, who is in a struggling school district, taking easy classes, and coasting to an A average. This boy is intellectually gifted, but he's distracted by his friends and sports and doesn't seem to try very hard in school. He has not yet thought about his goals for the future but has a vague notion of going to law school someday.

At face value, James is not getting the same high grades as Blake. But it is obvious that James is already working as hard as he can, and it is actually Blake who needs to be pushed or challenged to step up his game. As parents, we must consider the academic context, a child's effort, his abilities, and his goals when setting appropriate expectations for his grades.

Our expectations will also be informed by what we experienced ourselves. Two great questions to ponder:

1. What did you like (and may want to repeat) about how your parents dealt with academic expectations?

2. What did you not like (and want to make sure you don't repeat) about the way your parents handled academic expectations?

Where to Focus?

My (Peter's) worst grade in college came in an acting class. I needed a fine-arts credit, and my roommate convinced me to take Acting 101 with him. I've never minded public speaking, but I quickly found that getting into character and performing monologues was not my gift! To make things worse, I forgot about the only written exam in the course and showed up completely unprepared for the test. After bombing the exam, I had to rely only on my terrible acting skills to pull my grade up. In the end, I squeaked out a C. Aside from the ding in my GPA, I bumped into some real limitations in my gifts and abilities. Despite spending many more years in school pursuing advanced degrees, I made sure that was the last acting course I ever took.

Is it fair to expect good grades in every subject? There are times when a child is truly gifted in some areas but will struggle in others. Your son may be a natural artist and not a scientist. Or perhaps math comes easy, but he has a hard time with creative writing. These discrepancies in giftedness are sure to show up in his grades. How should parents react to that one C amongst the As and Bs on his report card? Ironically, a common approach to education involves identifying weaknesses and then focusing extra time and energy on these areas. Hiring tutors, taking extra study courses, and devoting all sorts of energy toward his deficits must be the solution. There is a case to be made for a student to address deficits in foundational skills that will keep them stuck or hinder growth, but do we balance this by also fueling his talents and gifts? Today's common approach can feel like punishment if we don't also allow enough time for our boys to pursue their passions. Chances are he won't major in English if he has no aptitude for it. If we as parents can keep a good perspective on the full purpose of school, perhaps we can find more tolerance for a marginal grade once in a while.

1. "What do you think is the goal of school?" Asking your son to think through and define his goals for school at a younger age will help navigate future conversations around school.

2. "What gets in the way of these goals?" Think through what your son's strengths and weaknesses are around school. How will these impact his academic experience?

3. "What helps you to be most successful at school?" Having your son name what he needs to be successful in school gives you an opportunity as parents to come alongside him to help him experience success instead of imposing rules for unclear purposes.

4. "How do you feel about our family's expectations about grades?" This invitation to dialogue gives you both an opportunity to share your thoughts on academics and hopes for the future.

Conversation 7

• • •

THE GIRLS TALK

Girls, Girls, Girls!

Girls may be the furthest thing from your tween boy's mind today, but don't be tempted to skip this chapter. It is only a matter of time before your son becomes sucked into the world of crushes, dating, and prom!

"What Is the Purpose of Dating?"

Various books and resources will give you lots of suggestions on when and how to set up dating rules and boundaries. The idea is you will release your son into the dating world slowly, perhaps starting with texts, selfies, or calls, then group dates, double dates, single dates, and who knows what other kind of interaction your son may suggest. Many young people these days don't even talk about *dating*. Instead, they "hang out," "go out," or "hook up" in a whole range of loosely defined and sometimes impulsive relational connections.

ARP *Adage*

Now is the time to decide how you will guide your child through the dating years—not later, when you are faced with an emotionally charged situation and are unable to think clearly.

Whatever the dating policy becomes in your home, it is best to begin by identifying your beliefs about the purpose of dating. Beginning with the big-picture objective will help you decide when your son is ready to begin the adventure of connecting with girls and what boundaries are needed to honor the purpose of dating.

"What is the purpose of dating?" is a fun question to ask young boys and usually generates a variety of responses. It is helpful to consider what you both believe dating will accomplish.

Following are some of the lessons I (Heather) hope our son will learn through his dating experiences.

Be a Good Friend

Most young boys (up to about seven years old) don't have a problem being friends with girls. Being a good friend of a girl involves the same rules as being a good friend to a boy. You share, take turns, listen, offer your ideas, invite them to join in play, encourage one another, and so on. Somewhere late in elementary school, however, boys can forget how to treat girls.

Young boys will use a variety of techniques to get the attention of a girl including flirting, teasing, ignoring, or even chasing. It is almost as if they wake up one day and look at girls through a new set of eyes and don't quite know the best approach for interacting with girls anymore. There is a new set of rules and social structures emerging in their world. Reminding sons how to be a good friend, ask questions, and be a good listener will help them practice their relational skills during the upcoming dating years.

Pursue Girls Graciously

Young men need to learn girls want to be pursued . . . not stalked, but pursued in a chivalrous way. Growing up in a home with older brothers, our family dinners were often interrupted by love-struck girls calling my brothers over and over again. I (Heather) saw how my brothers responded to this attention and learned I did not want to be a girl who chased the boys. I wanted to be pursued. Even after a first or second date, I would let the boy know he was going to need to initiate the call. This may have cost me a boyfriend or two, but I wanted to date boys who were willing to put some effort into the relationship.

Often boys don't know where to begin when pursuing a girl. They feel awkward and uncomfortable. Encourage your son to think about getting to know the young woman in whom he's interested, to learn about who she is and what she enjoys by being a friend and asking good questions. If she isn't interested in being a friend, she most likely isn't interested in being a girlfriend.

ARP *Adage*

Around sixth grade is when the phrase "going together" began to pop up in our home. I (Claudia) remember years ago when our sons started "going" with girls. Of course, they didn't go anywhere and rarely even talked to the girl they were "going with." Mostly, they wrote notes, so I guess you could say it helped their writing skills. Today, tweens connect through texting and social media rather than writing notes. They may have a new phrase for "going together," but the concept is the same: "I like you."

Be Respectful to Girls and Yourself

Our culture doesn't give boys many positive role models for how to talk with and about girls respectfully. Messages that girls are mere objects are subtly displayed through advertisements and more overtly portrayed in music, movies, and other media. It's easy for boys to see a girl and make comments to their friends about her body or appearance. Talking respectfully about a girl means looking beyond her appearance and seeing her as a person—a priceless creation—and not a mere object. This may require coaching your son how to handle situations when other friends are making comments that objectify a girl. How can he respond in a way that shows respect instead of joining in or just letting it slide?

Treating a girl with respect involves doing what you say you're going to do. If you promise to call or text a girl, you follow through. Boys also need to respect a girl by not sending her misleading messages. Many girls are easily wooed by a boy's attention. A respectful boy will give appropriate attention so a girl does not feel misled.

Learning about respect through dating can also involve respecting yourself enough to avoid or simply end unhealthy relationships. One friend told us a story of his fourteen-year-old son, Drew. Drew had spent several months getting to know Katelyn. She was a friend he had met through a church youth group. Drew and Katelyn texted and used social media to connect several times a day. They enjoyed meeting up at youth group and sitting near one another. He enjoyed her friendship, and she appeared to have many of the qualities he was looking for in a girlfriend: smart, hard-working, athletic, Christian, funny, and easy to be around.

Finally, Drew got the courage to ask Katelyn to be his girlfriend. She agreed, but it was like she switched into someone new overnight. Suddenly she started playing games with Drew—waiting long periods of time before responding back on her phone and acting quite cold. She even accused him of liking another girl and sitting too close to her. Drew was at a loss. He really liked Katelyn. He kept trying to figure out what he was doing wrong, texting more one day and less the next, sitting different places at youth group. Nothing seemed to make a difference. He couldn't figure out how to enjoy the friendship he had once shared with Katelyn.

Eventually, he figured out the respectful thing to do was have a conversation with Katelyn and let her know he really did like her and wanted to be her boyfriend, but only if she stopped playing these confusing games. He felt like his goal was to make Katelyn happy, but she kept moving or changing the goal. Katelyn was unaware of the way her behavior was affecting Drew and was unwilling to make any changes. With the help of his parents, Drew figured out Katelyn was probably just not ready for a dating relationship. He decided the respectful thing to do, for himself and Katelyn, was to return to being just friends again.

Be Honest

Dating can go on far too long when one or both people are not honest about their feelings. I want my son to be honest with a girl if his feelings have changed. Too often, people hold on to unhealthy relationships because they want to be sure to have a date for the upcoming dance, or they enjoy the attention they receive for dating a certain person. They may even be afraid to hurt a girl's feelings and continue to date for much longer than they are interested. Being honest when feelings have changed is part of learning to be a good boyfriend.

"When Can I Start Dating?"

This question may come up sooner than you think. And what will you tell your son? He can date when he's fourteen? Or when he's sixteen? Eighteen? Thirty? How about a group date? What about just hanging out with friends? Is that a date?

Setting dating restrictions until a certain age can be tricky. Some sixteen-year-olds are more ready to date than some twenty-two-year-olds!

Heather Flies, a junior high youth pastor with over twenty years of experience, has created some great questions for your teen son to consider in helping determine if he is "relationship ready":

1. Do I find my identity in Christ?

2. Do I have a healthy relationship with friends, especially people of the opposite sex?

3. Do I know what I'm looking for?

4. Do my parents trust me?

5. Will this relationship draw me closer to God?

We parents also have responsibilities in preparing our teens to date, starting with clearly stating our dating expectations and consequences. When you drive 45 in a 30-mile-per-hour zone, you know why the police officer is pulling you over. You also are expecting a speeding ticket. This is because you have clear driving expectations and consequences. Likewise, your teen needs to know clearly what is expected of him in dating and what will happen if he doesn't meet the expectations. Expectations to consider may include:

Who will you be with?

What will you plan to do?

Where will you go on the date?

When will you need to be home?

How will you get there and back?

As awkward as it may seem, parents have a responsibility to have frequent conversations with their tween about sex and sexual boundaries. Most parents report they have had *a* conversation with their son about sex and sexual boundaries, and yet most tweens will say the conversation never happened. This doesn't make sense—what's the disconnect? A young boy may not remember your birds and bees tutorial, or perhaps they just do their best to forget the uncomfortable experience of discussing sex with their parent. Some parents talk about the topic at such a high level, it never lands with their son. Keeping the lines of communication open about sex means talking about it on more than one occasion, in plain English.

Here are Heather Flies's questions for you, the parent, to consider if you are ready to help your tween navigate the world of dating:

1. Have you worked through your past relationship choices?
2. Do you have thoughtful reasoning behind your dating expectations?
3. Have you clearly communicated dating expectations with your young teen?
4. Have you had frequent (not just once), honest conversations about sex, sexual boundaries, and their impact on self-esteem, the future, and the heart?
5. Are you in-the-know concerning your child's friends, followers, and flirtations?

"Who Is Your Dream Girl?"

Just as your son is growing and becoming who God has created him to be, so are the young women he is meeting. What are the attributes of the woman you want your son to marry? Make a dream list and invite your son to make one too. Share your dream list with one another and talk about why you chose the attributes on your list. You can even combine your ideas into one agreed upon list of the characteristics he's hoping to find in a girl one day. Keep this document around so when your son is excited about a new girl, you can refer back to the list and see how she compares. This list can serve as his objective measuring stick in the future. Taking it a step further, have him brainstorm what kind of boy he needs to be to attract such a girl. What are the attributes he wants to have as a someday boyfriend?

My (Heather's) list for my son's future dates includes being respectful, positive, trustworthy, and faithful. If I'm going to trust a girl with my son, she better be trustworthy! She needs to understand that he deserves to be treated well. I've already been coaching our son to never settle or put up with chronic poor treatment from a girl he's dating—no matter how cute or popular she is. It is a two-way street, and boys need to understand their actions matter as well; he can set his own high standards of how to treat a girl and learn to honor her in a similar way.

I also believe I can model healthy relationship behavior in the ways I interact with the men in our household: my son and my husband. If I want my son to be attracted to a woman of high character, I need to show him firsthand what that looks like. I go out of my way to speak positively about his father and be an encouragement to my son. I've learned that boys and men may look tough and independent on the outside, but they crave affirmation and respect. As a mom and wife, I have to be intentional about communicating these messages because it is so easy to slip into a negative and critical posture in the stress of daily life.

In summary, the challenge as a parent is to be the healthy model of the very attributes you would like to see your children select in a future mate. Treat your spouse well, value your tween deeply, be trustworthy, and treat your son as a precious part of your life. Whether he knows it or not, he will begin to internalize these things as the norm for how relationships should work. If he bumps into a girl who doesn't treat him well, he'll more quickly recognize it and know there are better options available because he's seen it lived out in your home.

"Should We (the Parents) Meet Your Date? If So, When?"

Some may feel it is an outdated tradition, but many families have the expectation that when boys and girls begin to date, parents should meet the date. The date should come to your house and meet you early in the relationship. True, it may feel awkward and appear to be an intense requirement, but what does it communicate? To your son, it indicates that you care deeply about him and with whom he associates. It communicates that you have certain expectations for the girls he grants a deeper access to his life. To the girls, this requirement indicates that you are watching and monitoring what will happen in this relationship. It communicates that you care deeply for your son and will go to great lengths to protect and stand up for him.

Our friends, Angie and Chris, talked about their expectations with their sons, Michael and Patrick, and meeting the girls they were interested in dating. Angie and Chris made their home an easy place for their teen sons and their friends to hang out. The boys often host a gang of friends around a bonfire or even a night of games or movies. The boys knew that in order to ask a girl on a date, their parents had to meet her first. They didn't have to make it a formal event but could invite her to join in with other friends at their house. Angie and Chris gave Michael and Patrick plenty of space with their friends but would also interact with them throughout the evening. This allowed them to meet the girls before the boys would ask them out. As parents, watching the girls interacting with the other kids gave them a lot of information about how they carried themselves, dressed, flirted, or interacted with other boys. These observations were important as they discussed with their sons the pros and cons of pursuing a relationship with a particular girl.

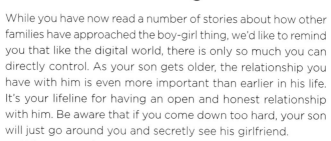

ARP *Adage*

While you have now read a number of stories about how other families have approached the boy-girl thing, we'd like to remind you that like the digital world, there is only so much you can directly control. As your son gets older, the relationship you have with him is even more important than earlier in his life. It's your lifeline for having an open and honest relationship with him. Be aware that if you come down too hard, your son will just go around you and secretly see his girlfriend.

When one of our sons was a senior in high school, he wanted to date a girl whose parents said no. (Their reasoning wasn't unsound; their daughter was four years younger than our son!) So what did these teens do? They slipped out at night to see each other. Were we horrified? Yes. Did we approve of this? No. Could we stop it? Not really, unless we wanted to stay up all night to monitor the doors and windows. What did we do? Let's just say our prayer life flourished during that time! We did all we could to prevent him slipping out while keeping our relationship with him intact.

Recently we were talking to a fifteen-year-old girl about boys, girls, parties, and so on. She told us, "Parents can't control everything, and overly strict parents will have sneaky kids." So as you're praying, pray for balance and realize that at some point you're going to have to trust your son. Look for ways to keep the relationship open and strong and also look for ways to build trust now. In the future, you'll be glad you did.

Sarah, a mother of a fourteen-year-old boy, told us how she had to lay down the law with her son after observing how his girlfriend acted in their home. The new girlfriend did not dress modestly at all and was overly flirtatious with their son, even in front of the family. She was not particularly respectful toward Sarah and seemed a bit over the top with her giggling and constant chatting. The final straw came when Sarah saw some of the inappropriate and suggestive texts this girl had been sending her son. She sat him down and basically said, "This is not going to happen!"

Another father we know is very clear about his approach for meeting his teen's dates. If his son (or daughter) wants to date someone in particular, they must make time for dinner with the family by the third date. He believes a family dinner together gives him an opportunity to see how this young woman interacts with his son and the other members of the family. A lot of one's character can be revealed during a meal together. Can she ask questions, listen to others, and hold a respectful conversation? Does she make eye contact, have good manners, and articulate sound opinions? This family dinner provides a hurdle for the son to consider. "Is this a girl I really want to invite over for dinner with my family?" If not, she probably isn't a great girl to date either.

"What Is Needed to Stay Pure?"

Guard Your Eyes

Most parents of tweens boys we talked to about the upcoming teen years shared a fear of their son being exposed to pornography. Today, with the number of devices our teens have access to, it feels impossible to shield teen boys from temptation. Your son may be exposed to pornography without even choosing it when a friend holds up a smartphone and says, "Have you seen this?" Unfortunately, statistics support these fears, with 93 percent of boys under age eighteen having been exposed to pornography. Of these boys, 70 percent have spent more than thirty minutes viewing at a time and 35 percent have watched thirty minutes consecutively more than ten times.[1] These numbers are shocking and sad. What can parents do?

Talking about pornography with your son may be tricky and uncomfortable, but it is important to discuss so he knows what to do when he is exposed to it. Often pornography is introduced when a peer shares a site or image they have found.

One friend shared a story of their twelve-year-old son and his first exposure to pornography. As a hockey player, Jake often rode a bus to and from his tournaments. On one occasion, a teammate passed his phone around the bus, sharing with all the boys pornographic images he had found on a website. Jake knew it was wrong and felt uncomfortable seeing it. He has a great relationship with his parents and knew he needed to tell them what had happened. Fortunately, Jake's parents reacted in a positive way. They told Jake they were proud of him for telling them. They didn't shame him for looking. They encouraged him to talk about how he felt and what he thought. Reminding him of the damage and destruction of porn addiction, they clarified the difference between porn viewing and porn addiction. Because he had seen this once did not mean he was going to need to continue to seek more images. Together they talked about calling the parents of the friend if this behavior continued, and they also talked about how Jake could decline to participate when the "phone passing" began on the bus. Jake felt empowered and agreed to let them know if this happened again.

Pornographic images can also be found quite by accident. When looking for an image for a research paper, your son may type an innocent web search and suddenly confront a variety

ARP *Adage*

One mom of a four-year-old boy shared, "Accidental exposure to pornography and inappropriate images can begin at a really early age. My four-year-old loves to play a particular game on my iPad. Recently I realized it had commercials interjected into the game. The game was age-appropriate, but the commercials definitely weren't! Periodically, I go through the settings and tighten them. You can't be too careful!"

of inappropriate images. Curiosity can take over, and before he knows it he is down a trail he never knew existed.

If your son hasn't had a conversation with you about pornography, he may not know how to bring up the subject or even what to call his experience. Giving him a vocabulary and understanding of where it comes from is important in combating pornography in his life. God created males to be visually attracted to females. Our bodies are designed to be beautiful to the opposite sex so we are drawn to one another. Unfortunately, this attraction has been used and abused to be something out of God's design. Pornography takes what God created for good and twists it to draw people into sin. Help him understand how destructive and sometimes addictive it can be so it doesn't become a negative force in his life.

Guard Your Heart

The Bible shows us how important our hearts are to God. In Proverbs 4:23 God commands us, "Above all else, guard your heart, for everything you do flows from it." The heart is the key to thoughts and feelings, which often lead to action.

Our culture carelessly uses the term *love* to mean desire, infatuation, attraction, or even fondness. Young boys easily

shift from, "I like her, I love her, I hate her, I love her again . . ."
This roller coaster is no fun for anyone. For teen boys, guarding
their heart means carefully choosing with whom and when to
share it. Once the heart is shared, the body will often follow. If
a boy believes he is "in love," he may use this excuse to justify
a number of choices he knows are not best for him and his future. Talk to your tween about going slowly and cautiously as
he begins to be attracted to girls. There is no rush! By seventh
or eighth grade, many boys will have witnessed enough junior
high romance drama that they can easily see the rationale for
holding off on dating for several more years.

Respect Yourself and Your Future Wife

Physical boundaries are important to establish and talk about
before challenging situations come up. One parent shared an
illustration of physical boundaries and an upcoming cliff. Imag-
ine sex is like a high cliff. There is a boundary fence twelve
feet from the edge. Curiosity about the other side of the fence
creeps in. There are friends on the other side talking about
their experiences. It's tempting to cross over the fence to get a
closer look at the view and see what all the hype is about. It's
easy to reason, *I won't get too close. . . . I'll be safe.* But sooner
or later, the edge just doesn't seem as dangerous as it once did,

ARP *Adage*

Adolescents can survive peer pressure much better when they
know what they believe and have decided beforehand on their
standards of action. However, even with this advance preparation, your son will at times be influenced by peers. But if you
are communicating with him and are majoring on the majors,
you can influence him today and build trust for the future.

and going right up to the very edge doesn't feel like a big deal. Dancing along the cliff's edge, flirting with danger, a fall is imminent. What is the right distance for the fence to be protective?

Remember, tween and teen girls are just as confused and misled as the boys! One twelve-year-old girl received the following email from a supposed friend, who also happened to be her boyfriend's sister, pressuring her to "get with it."

Dear Emily,

If I had a boyfriend I would not let this happen! You are not getting anywhere (holding hands, kissing, etc.). Drop the shyness when you are around my brother. I say this because it seems that when you are around other boys, you're not at all shy! Could you tell me why? Well, okay, it's not all your fault. I have told him off too. If I were my brother, I would have dropped you long ago, but don't worry, he won't. Here are some tips for you—hold hands, kiss, hug and talk to each other.

Stacy

P.S. Don't kill me!

As teens grow older, the pressure in boy-girl relationships only gets stronger. Dealing with a note like the one above is simple in comparison with being in a group where most of the other teens are already sexually active. A lot of teenagers start a sexual relationship only because of the peer pressure. Teenage moms who were asked why they started having sex almost all answer with reasons such as "I did not want to lose him" or "I was afraid to hurt him if I refused him." Add to the confusion the fact that some parents are neutral and others almost push their teenagers into sexual relationships, and it is easy to see how perplexing the relational environment of our teenagers has become. How can a parent help in the midst of this kind of peer pressure?

The sooner you start communicating, the better! Even at ten, eleven, or twelve, it's not too soon to be talking to your son. As awkward as it may be, talking with him about the pressure to become sexually active can open the communication lines and help sons decide what their own standards will be. Parents can be and need to be talking to their sons about sex. Consider the following statistics.

According to a survey commissioned by NBC News and *People* magazine of thirteen- to sixteen-year-olds, nearly 3 in 10 young teens are sexually active. Only 4 in 10 (41 percent) say they talk with their parents often about sex, while 62 percent say they talk to their friends about sex. Parents were also polled but there was a discrepancy; twice as many parents say these conversations about sex happen with their teens (85 percent to 41 percent).

These findings are enlightening for parents who are trying to help their adolescents cope with a promiscuous world. If we want our teens to have good, accurate, and value-based information, parents are the main source. We don't know any parents who say they want their teens to get their sex education from friends, movies, TV, and the Internet! These statistics encourage parents to talk to their kids about sex and be their main source for information.

God created each individual with a unique body, designed to be shared with their spouse in a holy relationship called marriage. Every time we share a part of our body with another, we can't take it back. After you hold someone's hand, you can't un-hold it. We give a bit of our body away when we let someone kiss or touch parts of it. This body isn't just yours. Song of Solomon says our bodies were meant to be shared with our beloved, not every cute girl along the way. This is difficult to understand when the hormones are surging and the message of culture says, "Just do it!" It is difficult as television and movies seem to make fun of those who choose to remain pure.

Our culture has normalized the idea of living together before marriage. Many of you may have friends or family members who are choosing to live together. Your son may already understand what this means or will begin to in the near future. He may have friends whose parents are living with someone who is not a spouse. It is not uncommon to see an aunt, uncle, or cousin in the family who is in an unmarried cohabiting relationship. Despite this trend of living together becoming the new norm, social scientists have consistently found couples who cohabitate before marriage do not fare as well.[2] Dr. Scott Stanley and his colleagues talk about the difference between "sliding and deciding" when it comes to marriage. Unfortunately, couples who live together without a marriage commitment tend to intertwine their lives. They rent an apartment, buy furniture, get a dog, intermingle their finances, and some even have a child. Pretty soon, they figure, "We might as well get married," as they slide into the biggest decision of their adult life.

Deciding to get married before cohabitating sends a very different message indicating "I choose you." The commitment levels, satisfaction, and long-term success of these marriages is significantly better. Having an open line of communication about your expectations regarding cohabitation is important to establish before the question becomes an option for your son.

Create Accountability

Remember when you were a teenager and out on a date? The emotions and nerves were on edge! When your son has a clear sense of what his boundaries are before he gets in a situation, he is better equipped to stick to his guns when the situation presents itself. Unfortunately, in some cases the pressure may

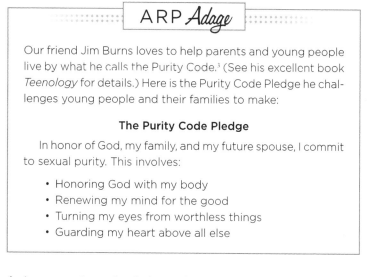

ARP *Adage*

Our friend Jim Burns loves to help parents and young people live by what he calls the Purity Code.[3] (See his excellent book *Teenology* for details.) Here is the Purity Code Pledge he challenges young people and their families to make:

The Purity Code Pledge

In honor of God, my family, and my future spouse, I commit to sexual purity. This involves:

- Honoring God with my body
- Renewing my mind for the good
- Turning my eyes from worthless things
- Guarding my heart above all else

feel too much, and it helps to know you have some external accountability in place.

Other programs, such as Passport2Purity by Dennis and Barbara Rainey, are a great way for parents to talk about purity and create accountability.[4] Some boys may even choose to wear a purity ring once they have made a commitment to remain pure.

Help your son come up with a ready response if he feels pressured into being sexually active. That classic line of thinking that says boys should initiate until the girls stops him might be reversed today with the girl the initiator. Perhaps your son can counter with "I'm choosing to wait" or "I'm just not comfortable with the responsibility of having a sexual relationship at this point."

As uncomfortable as it might be to talk about sex with your tween, let us encourage you to keep talking. Otherwise, their information comes from uninformed friends armed with misguided values, or from movies, television, and magazines that are totally unrealistic.

ARP *Adage*

Years ago, when *we* were in middle or junior high school, sex education went like this: Mom had the "big talk" with daughters and Dad had the "big talk" with sons—but that's ancient history. Serious big talks make kids uncomfortable; they often feel they are being preached at. They just don't work!

It is much better for the "big talk" to instead be many spontaneous and casual conversations. Talking in the car while driving to practice is more effective, and you'll find your son is more open and less embarrassed. When a neighbor's fifteen-year-old became pregnant, one mom had the natural opportunity to talk to her son about the risks of having sex. Mom pointed out that instead of having a typical carefree university experience, this girl would probably end up living with her parents or marrying a guy she doesn't even really know.

If you hear, "I know all of this already," and your kid tries to blow you off, just say, "I know you've heard this before, but I want to be sure you understand my views and I want to know your views. I really love you and I want to be confident that we're on the same page." When all is said and done, remember you are still your tween's major role model!

Now it is time for your conversation with your son. Talking about girls and purity may be uncomfortable for both of you. Try finding a comfortable setting where you might walk and talk. Go for a drive, take a hike, or plan a fishing outing as a more natural way to ease into the conversation and make it more comfortable. Some families choose to have a special weekend away together to talk about sex and purity.

You may feel like your son is too young to talk about some of the questions. Use your discretion, but be sure not to put it off too long. Often boys are thinking about girls or hear other boys talking about things long before parents realize it.

1. "What is the purpose of dating?" Talk together about why he believes dating is or is not important. Ask him what he thinks will be accomplished during dating. Share your thoughts with him about what you hope he will gain from dating.

2. "When can I start dating?" Ask your son what qualities or attributes he thinks makes someone ready to date. Share the list of questions from Heather Flies and discuss. Talk together about dating expectations and consequences.

3. "Who is the 'dream girl'?" Have fun creating a list of the attributes he is looking for in a girl. You can challenge

him to make a list of attributes he will want to embody so he can attract a great girl too!

4. "Should we meet your date? If so, when?" This question will give you some insight into what he is thinking about relationships too. You can share with him your expectations at an early age so he is aware when he does become interested in girls.

5. "What is needed to stay pure?" This question touches on many topics such as guarding your heart, guarding your eyes, respecting yourself and your future wife, being smart, and creating accountability. Think through what aspects you want to focus on. This may be a series of smaller conversations that come up naturally or as part of a special weekend away.

Conversation 8

• • •

THE MONEY TALK

Understanding Dollars and Sense

Tweens can think of all sorts of ways to spend their money, and our culture is constantly telling them what the next must-have item is. How can we as parents help our sons learn to be discerning with their money?

A good way to teach your tween the value of money is by encouraging him to earn some. When we (the Arps) lived in Vienna, Austria, our sons had a peanut butter business, and weekly would buy peanuts and make peanut butter. They were known as the Arp Peanut Brothers and their business motto was "100% pure peanut butter—we're all nuts for you!"

They kept track of what the peanuts cost, what they sold the peanut butter for, each son's time worked, and so on. The profit from this business enterprise was divided based on the amount of time invested in the business.

While this was a lot of work for us to supervise, and at times meant pitching in to help at cleanup, our sons learned valuable financial lessons.

An old Chinese proverb goes something like this: "To manage money, you have to have some money." Give your tween enough rope to let him experience spending his money foolishly. Gradually he will learn how to spend it in a reasonable way. Our sons learned how to manage money by having some money to manage and spend (sometimes unwisely!) while we were around to ask them, "And how did that work out for you?"

Why not have a brainstorming session with your tween and list ideas of jobs he might be interested in pursuing? Below are some of the ideas that one family came up with:

- Have a yard sale and get rid of old toys, clothes, etc.
- Grow tomatoes and cucumber and sell to neighbors
- Do yard work (mow grass, pull weeds, plant flowers)
- Water plants on a regular basis for neighbors
- Teach younger children a sport—soccer, tennis, basketball
- Provide the entertainment for birthday parties
- Baby-sit
- Take care of other people's pets when they are out of town
- Walk dogs
- Clean and organize attics and garages

"Where Does Your Money Come From Now?"

After hearing "We can't buy that because it costs too much money," a young boy suggested to his parents they should simply "use that little plastic card you always pay with." If only it were that easy! What a great representation of the misunderstandings children often have about money and how it works.

Your son has likely caught on to where his spending money currently comes from. Does he get an allowance or do you give him money whenever he asks? Does he earn his money by doing certain chores? Maybe he gets cash from grandparents on birthdays or holidays.

Personal spending money doesn't seem to matter that much to most young children under the age of nine or ten. But something happens as the tween brain begins to notice clothing trends and become more social. It takes significantly more money to join your friends for a walk to the mall, to buy a new shirt or video game, go to a movie, or eat out. Your tween son is now recognizing that more money in his pocket means more opportunities to go places, do things with his friends, and buy what he wants. As these activities increase, so do the requests for money. It can be exhausting (and expensive) for parents! But these growing requests for spending cash also present an opportunity to teach your son important concepts about budgeting, saving, spending, and setting goals.

Your son's inexperience with money means he doesn't have a good perspective to judge how much things should cost. Many tweens don't know if a house costs $50,000 or $500,000; they don't understand that a new car can easily be priced over $25,000; and they likely have no idea of your household income. Until they start handling money themselves, they can't really appreciate how it works.

We (the Larsons) found that our fourteen-year-old son began to understand money when he started earning it by doing chores around our neighborhood. Before this time, the only money he ever had was the money he was given. He would spend it on silly things, lose it, or give it away with almost no concept of its value. But when AJ began to earn his own money, he began to make better decisions, set some goals, and save up for the things he wanted.

The healthy shift that needs to take place is for the parent to move from "I earn and control all the money" to "You begin to earn some money and learn how to handle it." Your tween can start earning his own money by doing chores around the neighborhood, baby-sitting younger kids, or even setting up a garage sale. It is healthy for him to see what goes into earning money, and this understanding will definitely affect the way he spends.

As parents of three tweens, we began to notice the increasing desire and need our kids felt for cash in their pocket. But we were beginning to feel like walking, talking ATM machines. It was ten dollars for a movie, twenty dollars for a trip with friends to the mall, forty dollars for those athletic shorts "I must have. . . ." It never ended! Even athletic socks have become trendy and expensive. In an effort to avoid the constant requests for more cash, and the hope of teaching them the value of money, we decided to adopt a new strategy. We decided to increase the kids' allowance and give it to them once a month. The catch was this is all they would get. We would cover basics (like shoes and essential clothing needs), but they would need to budget for all activities or extras. If they wanted fancier shoes (or socks) than we were willing to buy, it was out of their pocket. Movies, five-dollar smoothies, trendy hats, and trips to the mall with friends would need to come out of their own monthly budget. If they didn't think they had enough, they could earn more by finding odd jobs or other creative ways to supplement their income.

When we went to this flat-rate monthly allowance system, our son quickly found a creative way to begin earning extra money so he could buy himself the upgraded smartphone he wanted. He started by trying to get some lawn-mowing jobs in our neighborhood, but didn't get much of a response. One of our neighbors, however, said he was sick of cleaning up in the yard after his two dogs. He offered to hire AJ for a weekly pick-up, and said he'd pay him twenty dollars per month. While there was nothing at all glamorous about this job, it was something our thirteen-year-old could do quickly and effectively, plus he'd already done this chore with our family dog. AJ recognized the opportunity and soon had ten households paying him monthly for this service. In just twelve weeks, he had his new phone. It was gratifying to see him thinking and acting more responsibly in the area of finances. It is also nice to avoid the role of parental ATM for the constant requests that had begun to emerge in our home.

We can't stress enough how important it is for kids to earn some of their own money along the way. It is just too easy to spend Mom and Dad's money, but the decision-making changes when it is your own hard-earned cash.

I (Peter) took a six-month trip abroad in college, and my father let me take his credit card "in case of an emergency." It was so easy and convenient to take out that little plastic card and charge those little extras (which added up to a big total). It started with a couple gifts for family, and then went to better food from nicer restaurants, and finally escalated to staying the weekend in an upscale hotel because I was so sick of the run-down dorms in which we'd been stuck for months. None of these things was "an emergency," but it was just so easy to spend *Dad's* money. I had to work through those decisions with my dad after the trip. Needless to say, this was the last time he handed me a credit card to use at my discretion.

When it is money I have earned, I'm typically very frugal and conservative, but somehow my financial personality completely shifted when it was Dad's money—not my own. How true is this for your children? We've seen a noticeable shift for many kids once they begin to earn their own money and set some goals for things they want to buy.

"What Things Do You Currently Need Money For?"

Is there any demographic more tuned in to fashion, music, and technology trends than our tweens? Corporate America's marketing experts understand how powerful the developmental pressures are for kids to fit in, own the right things, and wear the trendy clothes. So marketers now understand the science of using social media, celebrities, and advertising to create momentum around their products to drive tweens' spending habits.

One surprising example is what's happened with Starbucks. You wouldn't immediately think that twelve-year-olds care much about coffee. But a 2016 annual report from the investment firm Piper Jaffray looked at how teens are currently spending their money, and found some unexpected data.[1] Teen boys spend 20 percent of what's in their wallets at restaurants (with Starbucks at the top of the list). Another 15 percent goes toward clothing and 13 percent is spent on video games. Starbucks has a powerful brand, a prolific physical presence, and a savvy strategy. By adding sweet and frozen drinks to their offering and generating intrigue with tweens through "secret menu" items disseminated through blogs and social media, they've managed to drive a new wave of buying habits.

We definitely saw this shift as our tweens increasingly wanted to go to Starbucks and order whipped-cream-topped Frappuccinos on the way to school. Walking into middle school with a Starbucks drink is somewhat of a status thing. These requests for five-dollar specialty drinks was part of what drove us toward an allowance system that empowers the kids to spend their own

ARP *Adage*

Tweens would rather learn by experience than from the experienced—especially when it comes to money! Wise parents look for ways to allow their child to experience natural consequences.

money, even if it means they blow it all on what Mom and Dad think are over-priced and silly beverages.

As you consider this question about what you think your son really needs money for, think about the things you're willing to cover simply because you love and want to provide for your children. But also take time to think about the things your son could begin to buy for himself. How can you help him understand more of what it means to make good financial decisions?

"When Will You Need to Pay for Your Own Personal Expenses?"

Technology is advancing faster and faster, and our boys face growing demands for the latest and greatest smartphones and gaming systems. Pew Research reports a full 91 percent of teenage boys (ages thirteen to seventeen) either own or have access to a gaming system.[2] According to another study, 70 percent of thirteen- to seventeen-year-olds in 2013 owned a smartphone. That was up from 58 percent in 2012 and 36 percent in 2011.[3] That 70 percent figure from a few years ago has undoubtedly been surpassed. The most popular smartphones can cost over five hundred dollars and always come with a monthly bill to cover the talk, text, and data demands of the device. Who pays for all of this?

Most teens are excited to get their driver's license, so you can count on getting the question, "Can I have a car?" With the driver's license comes the need to insure a teen driver in your household, and with the car comes ongoing gas and maintenance. Nationwide Insurance surveyed almost fifteen hundred parents adding a teen driver (fifteen to nineteen years old) to their policy and found the average increase was eight hundred dollars per year. Are you ready for this? Have you and your spouse discussed what your plan will be?

At what age should a child gain access to the privilege of a smartphone or car? It may be a good idea to underline that word *privilege*, as these items truly are privileges to own. But with privilege comes responsibility. Circle the word *responsibility* and draw a line back to *privilege*. These two concepts are highly connected. There was a time when one earned privileges by showing themselves to be responsible. How you drive a car and use a phone are huge opportunities to prove yourself responsible. But as we mentioned in "The Technology Talk" chapter, our culture now gives kids all sorts of privileges with almost no expectations of responsibility.

There is not one right answer for every family. Some pay nothing for their teen's "extra" expenses, others pay everything. Depending on your resources, your own past experiences, and your child's personality, your answer to when your son should begin to pay for some of his own expenses will vary. The less you're willing to cover, the more likely the topic of getting a job will come up. Are you clear on when and if you'd like your tween/teen to get a job?

Being on the same page as parents and clearly communicating these expectations to your tween early on is important. The further the distance between expectations and reality, the more disappointment and frustration he will experience when reality hits.

"What Are the Financial Plans/Expectations for After High School or College?"

One couple, Skip and Leah, reflected on how they grew up in very different homes. Skip's father was generous and accommodating. For better or for worse, he was always there as a safety net to offer a second chance. He allowed Skip and his two older brothers to try many educational programs, live at home as long as needed, and provided financial help whenever they needed. As a result, it took many years for each boy to find true independence apart from the support of Dad. His generous support became a crutch that made it harder to launch. Skip was ten years younger than his oldest brother and began to notice this trend as he grew up. At some point, he realized he actually needed to cut his father off from supporting him any longer if he were ever to learn to stand on his own. Admittedly, that was a little backward and somewhat extreme compared with most young adults' experience. But loving, well-intentioned parents are everywhere; it is easy to overindulge one's kids without even recognizing it.

As Leah and her brothers grew up, her parents clearly informed each child they would have support for four years of college. At the end of the fourth year, whether they were finished with their studies or not, they would be cut off from all financial support. This meant no more help with a car, no moving back home, and no money when you get into a pinch. They had been informed (with four years' advance notice) to prepare to support themselves. Leah's parents followed through on this plan, and each kid stepped up to the plate to fully support himself or herself coming right out of college. They made sure they finished their majors, lined up jobs or internships, and had saved up for a reliable used car for transportation.

You'll need to decide what is the right amount of support for your children, but do them the favor of letting them know what to expect. While it might seem early to discuss some of these topics, the four short years from eighth grade to graduation will move faster than you think. Another key as parents is to make sure you get on the same page. This may take a while, especially if you come from very different home environments. Discussing these questions as a couple will help you prepare for the conversations you'll have with your son later on.

- What happens if he doesn't go to college? How much support is there after high school?
- Do you expect him to hold a part-time job during high school or college?
- How much of his own education, books, and room and board should he expect to pay for while in college?
- Can your adult son move back home if needed? For how long?
- How will you handle health insurance, student-loan debt, car insurance, etc., after college?
- In the long run, which is more loving: providing unending financial support or nudging him out of the nest?
- How did your parents handle financial support after high school and college? What would you like to repeat or not repeat with your children?

"If You Were Given $500 Right Now, What Would You Do With It?"

Buy a new phone? Put it in your savings account? Donate it to local disaster relief? This question is one of our favorites. It is a great way to end this money-talk conversation, and it is often quite telling. Not only is it enlightening to hear your son's dreams and wishes, but his answers can reveal an underlying approach to finances. There are three main things we listened for as we heard our kids answer this question.

Spenders vs Savers

Most individuals naturally fall into one of two categories: *spenders* or *savers*. Savers tend to view money as a source of security and don't like to wonder if they have enough to cover their expenses. If your son is a natural saver, you might hear him talk about buying one or two small things and tucking the rest into a savings account or his piggy bank. He may already have a goal he is saving up for, and this cash would go toward that special experience or item he has in mind for the future.

Spenders, on the other hand, view money as a source of enjoyment. They may live more in the moment and love to experience things today. Money tends to "burn a hole in their pocket." They are often willing to pay for others to share in their joy as well. Why wait if you can have it today? Why do it alone if you can share with others?

Either approach, spender or saver, can get out of balance if not monitored. It is good to begin to understand what type of financial personality your son has so you can help him avoid the pitfalls of becoming too extreme in either direction. Spenders can quickly dig themselves a hole as they make quick or poor decisions with their money. One passage from the Old Testament of the Bible says, "Whoever loves money never has enough; whoever loves wealth is never satisfied with their income" (Ecclesiastes 5:10). Spenders often feel like they never have enough money. They tend to live in a state of confusion and stress around money, wondering where it all goes.

Savers have their own pitfalls, yearning for a false security through money and missing out on the experiences life has to offer. Matthew 6:21 reminds us, "For where your treasure is, there your heart will be also." Truer words were never spoken; savers need to guard against this miserly notion of always trying to store up treasure for tomorrow. The more he saves, the more his heart can become consumed by it, never leading to a sense of contentment. Don't feel like you need to address all of this spender or saver talk today; this question will simply help you understand your son better as you anticipate future challenges he could face.

Spend, Save, Give

We were pleasantly surprised one year when AJ announced that he didn't want any birthday gifts. Instead, he wanted to have his eleventh birthday party at a local nonprofit that packed meals for those in need. He would ask his friends to make a donation in lieu of a gift and come help him pack meals. We knew he was a generous kid, but as parents we had not realized how mission-oriented his thinking had become, or how this would unfold in his decision-making. Now, four years later, he continues to give a good portion of his allowance to church and causes he cares about.

A second key topic this "What would you do with five hundred dollars?" question invites is a discussion about how income is allocated in terms of spending, saving, and giving. Listen if your son says anything about giving money to those in need or supporting a cause he cares about. Depending on your family's values and beliefs, you may have some strong opinions about giving a certain percentage to church, charities, or nonprofit organizations. It is never too early to begin teaching and modeling a generous approach to giving and sharing the wealth with which you are blessed.

Command those who are rich in this present world not to be arrogant nor to put their hope in wealth, which is so uncertain, but to put their hope in God, who richly provides us with everything for our enjoyment. Command them to do good, to be rich in good deeds, and to be generous and willing to share.

1 Timothy 6:17–18

An early discussion around how to allocate income between saving, spending, and giving can have a dramatic and lasting impact on your son. I've met adults in midlife who give away 10 percent, save 20 percent, and spend the remaining 70 percent. They often reference an early conversation with a parent who instructed them accordingly. By adopting this approach early, they've learned to live generously and within their means. This is so important as we live in a culture where 25 percent of American adults have no savings at all and the average credit card debt is over two thousand dollars.[4]

Conversation Idea

Tell your son your challenge is to have a special parent-son outing (between the two of you) and spend only ten dollars. Let him pick the place and see if the two of you can stick to the budget while you have this conversation about money.

1. "Where does your money come from now?" This is a simple conversation starter.

2. "What things do you currently need money for?" Find out what your son thinks he needs to spend his money on today.

3. "When will you need to pay for expenses related to a car, smartphone, clothes, food, or entertainment?" After talking with your spouse, ask your son what his expectations for these might be. Share with him your thoughts and expectations as well.

4. "What are the financial plans/expectations for after high school or college?" Although this seems light-years away, setting clear expectations at a young age will be a benefit in the future.

5. "If you were given five hundred dollars right now, what would you do with it?" Oh, what a fun question to explore with your tween. Share your thoughts too!

Online Resources:

www.kidsinthehouse.com
www.themint.org

THE BIRTHDAY BOX PROJECT

We hope you have enjoyed your conversations and activities with your son. The end of the tween years is only the beginning of the teenage years. Soon your son will be thirteen, and in five short years he will be eighteen, which is old enough to vote and the age when many kids leave home for college, the military, a gap-year service project, or enter the job market. Is he going to be equipped with the knowledge and skills he needs to live responsibly and independently? We (the Arps) used a five-year strategy we called the Birthday Box to help us prepare our sons for a successful launch.[1] It is really a plan of release that helps hand off new responsibilities and privileges each year, so by the time your son is eighteen he is ready to function on his own as an adult.

The Birthday Box

Becoming a teenager at our house was a big deal. But after the family celebration we planned another time to take our new teenager out to dinner with just the two of us. On this special occasion we tried to communicate the following message:

"We are excited about your growing up. You are now a teenager, and we want to relate to you on a more adult level. In five short years you will be eighteen and will probably be leaving for college. We want you to be prepared to make your own decisions, run your own life, and function as an adult. So, for the next five years, each year on your birthday we will give you new privileges and responsibilities for the coming year. This is progressive, and each year we will expand your privileges and responsibilities. Our goal is that by the time you're eighteen, you will achieve adult status and be able to make your own choices."

Then we introduced the concept of the "Arp Birthday Box" and presented our new teenager with a small wooden box filled with cards. On each card was a new privilege or a new responsibility for the coming year. A typical box for a thirteenth birthday might include areas similar to those covered in this book:

1. Curfew

2. Smartphones and Technology Privileges

3. Academics

4. Household Chores

5. Clothes

6. Money

7. Spiritual Life

While we didn't expect perfection with the Birthday Boxes, we did expect our teens to take them seriously and do their best. We gave them the following motivation: "If you manage your responsibilities well this year, then you'll move on to more privileges and responsibilities next year. Our goal is that you will be able to function as an adult by the time you leave home."

Then we gave each boy a projected plan of progression. We noted the progression across the page, which indicated independence at age eighteen. For each year we had projected new privileges and responsibilities illustrated in progressive boxes.

AGE	13	14	15	16	17	18
CURFEW	10 p.m.	10:30	11:00	11:30	Midnight	None
TECHNOLOGY						
ACADEMICS						
HOUSEHOLD CHORES						
MONEY						
SOCIAL LIFE						
SPIRITUAL LIFE						

*Parents: Feel free to create a chart like the above for your own Birthday Box plan. The categories and curfew examples are only suggestions. As you complete your own chart, think about your son's unique style, goals, strengths, and growth areas.

At that point, we discussed the coming year's box as well as the extended diagram. Nothing was in ink; all was negotiable. During this stage of life, we wanted our adolescent's input, and we wanted to work together. So, as our teens gave suggestions, we were willing to adapt our plan to the point all could buy in to it!

Warning! If the Birthday Box is only your input and your plan, don't expect your new teenager to jump up and down and go along with it! This is a cooperative effort! However, we did try to communicate the following:

"You can speed up this progression, or slow it down. Basically it's up to how you manage your Birthday Box. We don't think you're going to disappoint us. We're looking forward to watching you become a responsible adult."

How to Design a Teenage Birthday Box

First, you need an overall plan. However, the Birthday Box will be unique for each adolescent, as some teenagers are more responsible than others. Here are some areas to consider:

1. Curfew

We began at age thirteen with a curfew of ten o'clock one night per weekend. In addition, we needed to know where the teen was going and whom he was going with. Each year we added thirty minutes to the curfew, so by age seventeen the curfew was midnight, and by eighteen he set his own curfew.

Many parents say their thirteen-year-olds don't really need a curfew as they are seldom out at night. Even so, it is helpful to establish the principle of the curfew before it is needed. Then each year you extend the curfew. Your sixteen-year-old, whose curfew may be 11:30, does not feel as restricted because the curfew is thirty minutes later than when he was fifteen.

Our curfew was not an ironclad rule. We made exceptions for special events and school functions. Also, when a teen called home to let us know he was running late, we willingly added a few minutes. (We avoided most late-night adventures, but not all!)

2. Technology

A disclaimer: When our boys were teenagers, there were no cell phones, smartphones, tablets, or even home computers. Actually, we only had a land line, so tech privileges only dealt with phone usage. Today, screens are a major part of a teen's life. Smartphones are almost like another appendage—albeit in their back pocket. You need to decide together when it is appropriate to give your son more freedom in handling technology. His devices may include a phone, tablet, laptop, or even a smartwatch. We would suggest that you talk through this possible progression with your soon-to-be-teen. One beauty of the Birthday Box is sometimes what they want for this year, they see it will be part of their next Birthday Box and are able to defer gratification until then. That's actually a sign of maturity.

3. Academics/Homework

We began at age thirteen with limited supervision of homework and gradually worked toward their being totally responsible for their schoolwork. This was not the same age for each of our teens because some naturally took on schoolwork with more independence.

But by their junior and senior years in high school, homework was their business, even if they got their priorities mixed up, which they sometimes did. They learned a valuable lesson in managing their time—a lesson that benefited them as freshmen in college. Since they had already experienced being on their own academically, they were able to handle the freedom of college life.

LARSON *Adage*

When AJ was in sixth grade, we wanted him to learn to do his own homework and create an environment of independence. We bought him a desk so he would no longer have to work at the kitchen table. He knew we were still available to help him with homework as needed, but we didn't want to be running back and forth from his room to help him. Instead, we encouraged him to put a star next to a problem he needed help with and then move on until he had three stars. After three stars, we would come to help him with the work. During this time I was careful not to just show him how to solve the problem. Rather, I encouraged him to look in the textbook to see where he could see the concept being taught and solve the issue himself. If more clarity was needed, we might ask him to consider a homework website like Khan Academy to review the concept. Our goal was for him to be empowered and learn to discover where to go for help when he was struggling on math homework (instead of just Mom or Dad). We joked, "We won't be going off to college with you, nor will you want us to!" By October, he was doing all of his math homework independently.

4. Household Chores

The Birthday Box will include responsibilities, not just privileges. Consider what you want your son to know about managing a household as he launches out on his own at eighteen years old. Is it reasonable to think he'll be able to cook, do his own laundry, pick up the clutter, and take care of his things? Then build a progression into the Birthday Box. Perhaps it starts by keeping his own room clean. An occasional gift of a parent's helping hand will be appreciated, but sometimes it is better to close the door than to infringe on this agreement. Remember, this is a learning process.

In this area we (the Arps) had mixed results. One of our guys scored above average on housekeeping from the very beginning. Another lived in an unbelievable mess. Both finally got the picture: It's your responsibility, not ours. At least our boys knew how to do basic housekeeping jobs when they left home.

When is your son ready to wash and fold his own clothes? We also gave our boys the responsibility of caring for their clothes in their thirteen-year-old box. We have seen sweaters come out of the washing machine so small they looked like doll clothes, even though we cautioned, "Look at the label before you wash it. If the sweater has to be dry cleaned, we'll take it to the cleaners." We've also noticed pink underwear that had been white before it was washed with a maroon sweatshirt. Mistakes are part of the process. Too often college students bring their dirty clothes home for Mom to wash. We certainly didn't want this to occur!

5. Money

Some teens have a built-in knack for managing money; others have a knack for spending it! We started by letting our teens manage their money for school supplies and lunches. Once they showed signs of maturing, we added shopping for clothes, and progressed from weekly allowances to monthly allowances.

We also included expectations about part-time and summer jobs in this area. At thirteen, one teen mowed yards during the summer. At fourteen, two of our teens worked as counselors at a Scout camp. It can be difficult for teens to get a steady job until they are sixteen, but we felt they learned much through these working experiences.

Again, the standards we set varied for each teen. With all the extracurricular activities, one teen simply could not work and still complete schoolwork. Working, however, kept another busy and out of trouble. Obviously the teen's responsibilities at home will be less if he is working.

If your son begins to work regularly, consider letting him open a bank account. You may want to suggest that a certain percentage of the money he earns be saved for college or a special purchase. (You could include this standard as a part of the Birthday Box.)

6. Dating and Parties

To offset disappointment at not being able to date right away at thirteen, we put a tentative plan in their Birthday Boxes for when they could progress to group activities at fourteen and fifteen and finally a single date at sixteen. Seeing that these privileges were just around the corner kept them from complaining too much. With parties, we initially wanted to know where they were and what adults were supervising. It helped that our teens could not yet drive so we were involved in the logistics. As they grew older, we loosened up on needing to know everything, but we still enforced the curfew. You'll have to make decisions around dating and parties that reflect what's best for your son.

7. Spiritual Life

While you can't legislate what your teenager will or will not believe, you can influence him! You can provide reading material—but forcing him to read it may prove counterproductive! In the early teen years we tried to help our boys find interesting devotional material on their level. Check out your local Christian bookstore for devotional books and books on Christian beliefs and values. We did include in the Birthday Box reading at least one faith-based book each year. We also subscribed to a relevant cutting-edge Christian magazine for teens. No doubt there will be apps, blogs, or websites your son will also relate to. Ask his youth leader for some suggestions.

We also included attending a youth conference or a church youth group ski trip in our boys' boxes. The youth group at your church can be a positive influence. But what if your teenager hates the youth group? We know some families who changed churches during the teen years just to find a good youth group for their adolescents. One mom included the privilege of choosing a church in the box for her son's fifteenth birthday because the son was very unhappy at the family's church. That year the son became very active in church for the first time simply because of his new excellent youth group.

Again, developing a plan when the teen is young and still receptive to parental input ensures a gradual transition from parent's to a teen's own values and convictions.

8. Driving, Meal Preparation, and So On

Driving is a big privilege for a teen and often requires a full-fledged agreement within the Birthday Box. One parent in a group we facilitated drew up the following contract together with his son.

Kyle's Driving Contract

Seat Belts

- I must wear a seat belt when I drive, and so must any passengers.

Passengers

- No more than two people in the front seat (including me).
- No more than three people in the back.

Driving Range

- I can drive only within a twenty-mile radius, unless accompanied by an adult.

Maintaining Grades

- Grades must stay above a B average.

Consequences of Breaking Contract

- If grades are below a B average, the car is taken away for all social events until grades improve.
- Any speeding or parking tickets I get, I pay for myself.

Miscellaneous

- No texting or using phone while driving!
- I will always let my parent know where I'm going to be.
- No one else shall drive the car.
- No one under the influence of alcohol may ride in the car. (We realize exceptions can happen when the only safe way for the teen to get home is to become the designated driver, but we would encourage parents to have the general guideline to not allow friends who are drinking to ride with them.)

One Mom's Experience

We had a driving contract for our son, Leif, but he was not excited about it. He told us he polled three people at school and they all thought it was "lame." I asked him who he polled, and he said that was confidential information. He was so mad about the contract that when he got it, he read through it like an attorney. Then he said, "I will sign it but I will not date it." He had to have the last word. We still have an undated contract, but it is still in place. And to this point, he has had no accidents.

You may also want to include other areas in your teen's Birthday Box, such as simple car mechanics or getting a certification in CPR. You might want to include reading a book about investments and making a first small investment in the stock market. Whatever areas you choose to include, the goal is the same: to develop the teen's competence to function productively in the adult world.

At the end of this chapter you will find a guide to help you design your own plan of release.

Monitoring the Box

Plan a quarterly or six-month evaluation with your teen to discuss how he is doing. If your son lacks self-discipline, you may want to get together more often.

One of our sons kept asking, "How am I doing?" Since he was doing very well, we hadn't mentioned the box. After his comment, we realized he needed some positive feedback, so we began commenting occasionally, "You're doing a great job of keeping up with your homework."

What if your son doesn't carry through with the responsibilities or abuses the privileges? If he fails in one area, just repeat that area the next year. Remember, your teen wants new privileges. Once he understands they are accompanied by responsibilities, we hope he will not let you down.

One of our teenagers was the classic academic underachiever, even though he was bright, so we made achieving a B average a requirement for getting his driver's license.

"Gee, Mom, I grew up in Austria. You can't drive there until you're eighteen, so it's no big deal," he replied.

When his friends began to get their licenses, his attitude changed. Suddenly his grades began to improve.

With one son, we found we needed to be flexible. Once we saw improvement in his grades and his attitude toward his studies, we allowed him to get his license, even though he did not have a B average. But his driving was limited to work and to youth activities. A year later he finally achieved a B average, and we received the good student discount on our insurance.

A caution: Before you tie grades into privileges, ask yourself, "What is reasonable for my teen?" Some kids work harder to maintain a steady C average than others do to make straight As.

Our teens knew that their progress toward new freedoms depended upon four factors: overall attitude, spiritual growth, academics, and how well they managed the box.

Excelling in an area can speed up some privileges. For instance, if your son from an early age has been a good manager of finances, he might have his own debit card earlier than another sibling.

Alternative Approaches

You may want to begin the Birthday Box at eleven or twelve, or perhaps your teen will enjoy the box at thirteen, but not again at fourteen, or will not cooperate if the Birthday Box is begun at fifteen. Some of the parents in our parenting groups and seminars adapted it as a High School Box with freshmen, sophomore, junior, and senior privileges and responsibilities.

One mom learned about Project Thirteen (discussed earlier in this book) and the Birthday Box right before her son's fourteenth birthday, so she combined the two. The important thing is to set up a well-defined, progressive structure for increasing responsibilities and privileges each year.

Fourteen-year-old Ryan's Steps to Adulthood

1. You may choose your own clothes.
2. Your homework will no longer be supervised, but we will be glad to help if asked.
3. Your bedtime is extended until 10:30 p.m. on school nights.
4. You will receive a $50 allowance per month for spending money and school obligations. Extra money may be earned by doing yard or housework.
5. Your room is your responsibility. Mom has the right to refuse to allow friends to visit if your room isn't clean.
6. You are responsible for the care of your clothes. Mom will teach you how to wash, dry, and fold your clothing.

I know you can do it. I love you.
Mom

Ryan hung the document on his bedroom wall and worked hard to achieve these responsibilities. But our friend's story doesn't end there. When Ryan's sixteen-year-old brother, Cody, celebrated his birthday, their mom took Cody out to dinner and discussed what he still needed to learn before he left home in approximately twenty-four months. Together they made a list, and now he is taking care of his clothes and, among other things, learning how to cook basic foods.

Her nine-year-old son, Matthew, watched this process and decided to get a head start. That summer he listed his own goals, one of which was to "place" in an event in the city swim meet. He not only placed in several events, but also received the Most Improved Swimmer award for his local swim team.

"Matthew was the only swimmer in our club that made and met his personal goals," his coach told his mother at the awards dinner.

Why Not Take a Chance?

Wise parents begin working toward their offspring's independence almost from the moment the child is born. Just as you hand the baby a spoon for eating, knowing he or she will probably plaster the wall with food, so you take risks all along the journey. Releasing areas of responsibility can eliminate much frustration for both the teen and parent as you progressively increase freedom when your son demonstrates responsibility. Why not take the chance? Go on and give your adolescent a Birthday Box!

Establishing Teenage Birthday Boxes

1. Brainstorm your categories and list all the things your son needs to know in each area before he leaves home.

2. By each area put when you think he will be ready to assume the responsibility.

3. Sketch or type two box diagrams. Insert the different areas and potential progression on each copy and give one to your son.

4. Be open to discussion. Let your son co-create his Birthday Box progression. Once you've agreed on your plan, remain open to annual tweaks that may need to take place.

5. Get him an actual Birthday Box container and present him with the first year's challenge cards and the diagram of the overall plan. Each year on his birthday, present him with a new set of cards for that year. Review, refine, and celebrate his progress!

6. Keep the following questions in mind:

   A. Am I releasing too much or not enough freedom to my son?

   B. Am I giving him too much or not enough responsibility?

It takes a lot of work to work yourself out of a job! We hope the concepts discussed in this chapter and throughout the book will give you a context for healthy conversation and intentional parenting. We don't have all the answers, we don't know your child's particular strengths and weaknesses, and we can't anticipate all the curve balls our culture will throw at your family. Still, these principles of responsibility, freedom, and privilege are timeless and reflect the journey of basic human development.

Remember, while today may feel overwhelming, these years of parenting your son will quickly pass you by. It may not always feel pleasant or easy as your son navigates the daily challenges of the teen years. But before you know it, you'll be looking up at your tall son and watching him climb into the driver's seat of his car as he heads off to work or school. He will be equipped for adulthood. Enjoy the journey, be grateful along the way, and keep the perspective that your efforts now will equip him for a lifetime of healthy independence.

NOTES

Conversation 1: The Big-Picture Talk

1. Drew Desilver, "In the U.S. and abroad, more young adults are living with their parents," Pew Research Center, May 24, 2016, http://www.pewresearch.org /fact-tank/2016/05/24/in-the-u-s-and-abroad-more-young-adults-are-living-with -their-parents/.

2. James Dobson, "Some Battles with Adolescents Not Worth Waging War," *The Knoxville News-Sentinel*, October 31, 1998, B4.

Conversation 2: The Friends Talk

1. Lisa Damour, "The Emotional Whiplash of Parenting a Teenager," *New York Times*, July 13, 2014.

2. Derek Thompson, "How Teenagers Spend Money," *The Atlantic*, April 12, 2013.

3. John Eldredge, *You Have What It Takes* (Nashville: Thomas Nelson, 2004), 3.

4. Mary Pipher, *Reviving Ophelia* (New York: Ballantine Books, 1995), 83.

5. P.T. Costa Jr. and R. R. McCrae, *Revised NEO Personality Inventory (NEO-PI-R) and NEO Five-Factor Inventory (NEO-FFI) Manuel* (Odessa, FL: Psychological Assessment Resources, 1992).

6. Merton and Irene Strommen, *Five Cries of Parents* (New York: Harper & Row, 1985), 6.

7. Josh Wiley, "Bible Verses About Friendship: 20 Good Scripture Quotes," What Christians Want to Know, May 1, 2011, http://www.whatchristianswant toknow.com/bible-verses-about-friendship-20-good-scripture-quotes/.

Project Thirteen

1. Adapted from David and Claudia Arp, *Suddenly They're 13—Or the Art of Hugging a Cactus* (Grand Rapids, MI: Zondervan Publishing, 1999).

Conversation 3: The Body Talk

1. Dave Walsch and Erin Walsch, *Why Do They Act That Way? A Survival Guide to the Adolescent Brain for You and Your Teen* (New York: Atria, 2014).
2. Daniel Siegel, *Brainstorm: The Power and Purpose of the Teenage Brain* (New York: Penguin, 2013). Dr. Siegel also shares his insights on the teenage brain in a video found at https://www.youtube.com/watch?v=kH-BO1rJXbQ.
3. "Research on Males and Eating Disorders," National Eating Disorders Association, https://www.nationaleatingdisorders.org/research-males-and-eating-disorders. See also "Eating Disorders in Adolescent Males: An Interview with Dr. Mark Warren," Maudsley Parents, http://www.maudsleyparents.org/boys.html.
4. "Eating Disorder Symptoms and Effects," Timberline Knolls Residential Treatment Center, http://www.timberlineknolls.com/eating-disorder/signs-effects/.

Conversation 4: The Technology Talk

1. Ben Horowitz, "NY Teen Rachel Canning Agrees to Dismiss Lawsuit Against Her Parents," *NJ Advance Media*, March 18, 2014, http://www.nj.com/morris/index.ssf/2014/03/case_ends_as_nj_teen_agrees_to_dismiss_lawsuit_against_her_parents.html.

Conversation 5: The Faith Talk

1. James W. Fowler, *Stages of Faith* (New York: Harper & Row, 1981).
2. Warren Benson, *The Complete Book of Youth Ministry* (Chicago: Moody Press, 1995), 53.
3. B. Griffen and K. Powell, "I Doubt It: Making Space for Hard Questions," *Stickyfaith.org*, March 10, 2014, http://stickyfaith.org/articles/i-doubt-it.
4. Jim Candy, Brad M. Giffin, and Kara Powell, *Can I Ask That?* (Pasadena, CA: Fuller Youth Institute, 2014).

Conversation 6: The Academics Talk

1. CareerBuilder, August 18, 2011, www.careerbuilder.com/share/aboutus/pressreleasesdetail.aspx?id=pr652&sd=8/18/2011&ed=8/18/2099&siteid=cbpr&sc_cmp1=cb_pr652_.
2. K. E. Ablard and W. D. Parker, "Parents' Achievement Goals and Perfectionism in Their Academically Talented Children," *Journal of Youth and Adolescence*, 26, no. 6 (December 1997): 651–67.

Conversation 7: The Girls Talk

1. Luke Gilkerson, "Teens and Porn: 10 Stats You Need to Know," August 19, 2010, http://www.covenanteyes.com/2010/08/19/teens-and-porn-10-stats-your-need-to-know/.
2. S. M. Stanley, G. K. Rhoades, and H. J. Markman, "Sliding Versus Deciding: Inertia and the Premarital Cohabitation Effect," *Family Relations* 55 (2006): 499–509.

3. Jim Burns, *Teenology* (Minneapolis: Bethany House Publishers, 2010), 80.

4. Dennis Rainey and Barbara Rainey, *Passport2Purity* (Little Rock, AR: FamilyLife Publishing, 2012).

Conversation 8: The Money Talk

1. "Taking Stock With Teens, Spring 2016 Infographic," Piper Jaffray, April 13, 2016, http://www.piperjaffray.com/2col.aspx?id=178&releaseid=2156896.

2. Amanda Lenhart, "A Majority of American Teens Report Access to a Computer, Game Console, Smartphone and a Tablet," Pew Research Center, April 9, 2015, http://www.pewinternet.org/2015/04/09/a-majority-of-american-teens-report-access-to-a-computer-game-console-smartphone-and-a-tablet/.

3. "Ring the Bells: More Smartphones in Students' Hands Ahead of Back-to-School Season," Nielsen, October 29, 2013, http://www.nielsen.com/us/en/insights/news/2013/ring-the-bells-more-smartphones-in-students-hands-ahead-of-back.html.

4. "American Family Financial Statistics," July 9, 2014, http://www.statisticbrain.com/american-family-financial-statistics/.

The Birthday Box Project

1. Adapted from David and Claudia Arp, *Suddenly They're 13—Or the Art of Hugging a Cactus* (Grand Rapids, MI: Zondervan Publishing, 1999).

Peter J. Larson, PhD, is a licensed clinical psychologist and currently works at Gloo, Inc. He is the coauthor of the PREPARE/ENRICH Customized Version and the Couple Checkup Inventory and book. Heather Larson, MS, has her master's degree in psychology. She is the founder of Bridgewell Coaching and works as a Christian relationship coach. She and Peter regularly teach and speak together. They are the hosts of the *10 Great Dates Before You Say "I Do"* DVD curriculum. The Larsons have been married for more than twenty years and have three children.

Claudia Arp and David Arp, MSW, are founders of Marriage Alive International, a groundbreaking ministry dedicated to providing resources and training to empower churches to help build better marriages. The Arps are authors of numerous books and video curricula, including the *10 Great Dates* series, *The Connected Family*, and *Suddenly They're 13—Or the Art of Hugging a Cactus*. The Arps have appeared on the NBC *Today Show*, CBS *This Morning*, PBS, and *Focus on the Family*. Their work has been featured in publications such as *USA Today*, the *Washington Post*, *New York Times*, *Wall Street Journal*, and *Time* magazine. When they are not writing or speaking, you'll probably find them hiking trails in Northern Virginia, where they live, or in the Austrian Alps, where they love to hike. For more information, visit www.10greatdates.org.

The Companion Book for Parents of Daughters

This parallel to *He's Almost a Teenager* hones in on the specific needs of girls, showing you how to be there for your daughter during the critical tween and teen years. Offering the tools you need to start essential conversations now, *She's Almost a Teenager* will help you discover what your daughter really thinks about boys, school, God, and her future. Based on tried-and-true parenting wisdom, you will find thoughtful questions and talking points that lead to natural, meaningful conversations on key issues, including:

- Physical and emotional changes your daughter is facing
- Taking ownership of her spiritual life
- Using social media responsibly
- and much more

Don't miss the opportunity to connect with your daughter when she needs you the most.

"Want girls who learn to think wisely and confidently tackle life? Learn from the profound and practical question-asking guidance offered in this book."
—**Jim and Lynne Jackson**, co-founders of Connected Families

She's Almost a Teenager by Peter and Heather Larson & David and Claudia Arp

BETHANYHOUSE

Stay up to date on your favorite books and authors with our free e-newsletters. Sign up today at bethanyhouse.com.

Find us on Facebook. facebook.com/BHPnonfiction

Follow us on Twitter. @bethany_house